BERNARD CODD

HIS RACING STORY

By

PAUL SKINNER

First Published
April 2023

Printed by Chris Cook Print

CC PUBLISHING

About the Author

Paul Skinner comes from Old Leake in Lincolnshire and works in the building trade. He is a fan of motorcycle racing, in particular a golden era for British riders and manufacturers, the 1930s to the 1960s. This was a time when a handful of Lincolnshire riders were competing with - and beating - the best riders in the world.

Taking great interest in their exploits, Paul was always on the lookout for information or books about these popular Lincolnshire racers who, between them, scored many short circuit, continental and TT wins, often whilst also competing in local scrambles and trials competitions. It soon became apparent that there were no books, so he took it upon himself to record the careers of these popular local heroes himself.

This book is the follow up to Paul's first publication, *Austin Munks – Diary of a Motorcycle Racer*.

Look out for further titles in the future.

Dedication

In memory of my late parents, Noel and Doris,
who gave me the best possible start in life, taught me old fashion values,
and prepared me for the real world.

Contents

Introduction & Acknowledgements

Foreword

Chapter One: How it all began	Page 1
Chapter Two: Road racing	Page 5
Chapter Three: A brief history of Cadwell Park	Page 19
Chapter Four: 1956	Page 31
Chapter Five: Isle of Man Clubmans TT	Page 43
Chapter Six: Short Circuits and the Manx	Page 63
Chapter Seven: Scarborough International	Page 85
Chapter Eight: 1957	Page 103
Chapter Nine: The Golden Jubilee TT Races	Page 127
Chapter Ten: A typically wet Cadwell Park	Page 141
Chapter Eleven: Crystal Palace	Page 169
Chapter Twelve: The long road to recovery	Page 175
Chapter Thirteen: Bernard's adversaries	Page 181
Chapter Fourteen: Life after racing	Page 187
Postscript: The TT-winning BSA 350 Goldstar	Page 192
Afterword	Page 193

Introduction and Acknowledgments

While researching and writing my first book, *"Austin Munks - Diary of a Motorcycle Racer"*, Bernard Codd's name appeared frequently in reference to his short, but very successful and promising motorcycle racing career.

In 2007 I was fortunate enough to meet Bernard and was privileged to listen to his fascinating stories regarding his connections with Austin Munks, Sam Coupland, Geoff Duke, and Dickie Dale - to name but a few from that magical era of motorcycle racing in this country back in the 1950s. He was always prepared to answer questions and recall memories of those halcyon days with such enthusiasm, and you could see it was an important and special time in his life. I decided then that - as with Austin Munks - Bernard's story needed to be told and put on record for the future as, in my opinion, it plays an important part in motorcycle road racing history as well as our local history.

Some of you will be familiar with his name, but few with his achievements so this is his racing story as best as I can discover it. After reading it I think you will agree that there is no doubt Bernard certainly had the natural ability and that, with the right machinery, the right backing, the right encouragement, and a bit of luck, he had the potential to have been up there with the motorcycling greats of our country.

Much of the information in the book has been sourced from newspaper reports but some of the results are from race day programmes that I have collected over the years, so these are only as accurate as was possible on the day to scribble them down, so mistakes may have been made. There will also be information I have failed to discover; some unfortunately lost forever but that (I think) makes what I have discovered even more important.

As with any project like this you can't succeed without assistance from other people (and, at times, 21st century technology), so I need to thank the following people for their help. First and foremost, I need to thank Jane Codd for not just giving me her blessing to write the book but lending me her personal photographs and allowing me access to a scrapbook that Bernard's mother put together at the time, which enabled me to answer some of the questions I came across.

Being able to access the National Newspaper Library's on-line archives was not just informative but fascinating, and I also need to thank Boston Library for their assistance and the use of their photocopying facilities. John Almond once again has been invaluable in identifying people in photographs and supplying photographs used in the book. Paul Taylor corrected me on technical and mechanical accounts which were way beyond me. Andrew and Jane Carrott were not only responsible for proofreading and editing the book but have also guided me through what has, at times, taken me out of my comfort zone. The staff at Chris Cook Print also deserve a mention for their patience and for turning my ideas into reality.

Newspapers I have sourced information from, both on-line and in original paper form, are:

Louth Standard, Boston Guardian, Lincolnshire Standard, Skegness Standard, Yorkshire Post, Yorkshire Evening Post, Leeds Mercury, Sleaford Gazette, Spalding Guardian, Daily Herald, East Kent Times and Mail, Newark Advertiser, Nottingham Evening Post, Peterborough Citizen and Advertiser, The Croydon Times, The Grantham Journal, The Dundee Courier and Advertiser and the Cambridge Daily News.

FOREWORD

Written with a passion for local sporting history, this book has not only captured the story of Bernard's remarkable journey but also gives a wonderful snapshot of the post-war motorcycling community during the golden era for British motorsport. Thank you so much, Paul.

Growing up around Bernard I was always aware that he had achieved something special. His cabinet, which held shiny and exotic-looking trophies seemed magical and the motoring books, magazines, and photos deposited around the house were also a constant reminder of his passion. It was only when I became an adult that I came to fully understand the bittersweet story of his meteoric rise, his hopes, his dreams, and then the disappointment of a career-ending injury. Despite this he was always enthusiastic and positive about his adventure, his eyes sparkling as he excitedly recounted stories of the people, the places and the races.

This experience also translated into him becoming my greatest supporter, encouraging me to give everything in life a go so that I would have a chance of capturing my dreams as he did as a young man, and for that I am forever grateful. Most of us can only dream of touching such success in our lives. Bernard achieved it.

He was - and will always be - my hero.

Nick Holt (Bernard's Godson)
Horncastle, Lincolnshire

Note regarding race results:

This book features race reports that include results where available, and uses the following convention:

Position Rider (Motorcycle) Race Time, Average Speed, Prize Money

CHAPTER ONE

HOW IT ALL BEGAN

"Tell him to come and see me"

Bernard David Codd was born on 20th June 1934 to Mr and Mrs D.H. Codd, a farming family from Wrangle, a small village on the Lincolnshire coast. Bernard had two brothers and a sister, and his father introduced him and his brothers to motorcycling by taking them to post-war meetings at Cadwell Park, where Bernard would collect discarded lemonade bottles and cash them in at the caterer's tent.

His first experience of riding motorcycles was on a machine that had been made up of bits and pieces from a 1927 Ariel and a Triumph. This bike had been built by Dave Smith from Croft who was soon to marry Bernard's elder sister, Barbara. With the wedding day fast approaching Dave decided to give up riding and so gave the machine to Bernard. This was soon followed by a JAP-powered OK Supreme.

Bernard immediately took to motorcycling. He would borrow straw bales from his father's barn and on Sunday mornings he and a group of his friends could be seen and heard racing up and down the miniature grass track they had marked out in one of the family's fields. Bernard and his brother Arnold would time each other racing round the course.

Bernard was educated at Boston Grammar School and in his early years was a keen table tennis player, winning numerous trophies. On reaching sixteen Bernard's father bought him a new 350cc AJS.

Bert Stones (one of Bernard's neighbours) would watch the boys riding round the field and, in a casual conversation, told Austin Munks (the garage proprietor from the nearby village of Leverton who was sponsoring Dickie Dale, another local rider at the time) about this lad who was always playing about on motorcycles. *"Tell him to come and see me"* was Austin's response. At that time Austin had two trials motorcycles, a 197cc James and a Norton 500T, and soon Bernard was riding one of them in club events. His first outing, in 1950, was at Lincoln where he finished 17th.

Bernard went into the RAF in 1952 to do his two years of national service as a transport driver. During this time, he won a first-class award in one of the service events and found the time to compete in trials events at the weekends. Back in civilian life he went on to win many trials events.

As I am concentrating in this book predominately on Bernard's road-racing career I have limited the number of trials events to a few of the more interesting and important reports. Not only that, but these local events weren't very well documented and are difficult, if not impossible, to track down. One report in the Lincolnshire Standard dated 14th February 1953 states that The Boston Motorcycle & Light Car Club held their fourth annual dinner and dance at The White Hart Hotel, Boston on Tuesday 10th February. At this time the club had 100 members and the President was R.H. "Dickie" Dale. The awards were presented by Mrs H.H. Watson, to the following recipients:

Annual Sports Cup
Winner - G.R. Brown
Runner-up - J. Adams

Valentine Cup (team trial)
Winners - Mr Brown, Mr Goodliffe, and Mr Grief
Runners-up - B. Kime, A. Kime and B. Codd
W.P. Maidens Cup (grass track aggregate)
Winner - P. Watkin
Runner-up - J. Walker

Holland Challenge Cup
(in memory of the club's first president, Mr Chas Holland)
Winner - Mr. N. Wainer
Runner-up - Mr. J.A. Minns

On Saturday 28th February 1953 Bernard won the Peterborough Motorcycle Club's "Stuffins Trophy" trial on his 500cc Norton.

Later in the year Bernard took part in the Lincoln club trial riding his 197cc James, finishing third behind K. Frith from Hagworthingham on a similar machine, and the winner was T. Organ on another lightweight.

Bernard was unable to get leave from the RAF in February 1954 to compete and defend his win in the "Stuffins Cup" held at Peterborough, but there was some consolation as it was won by his brother, Arnold. Bernard did, however, get time off from his national service duties to compete in Banovallum Motorcycle Club's first sporting trial of 1954 held later in the month on Sunday, February 21st at Winceby. M. Frith (197cc James) from Hagworthingham won losing 98 marks, second was T.A. Organ (197cc OEC) losing 102 marks, with Bernard (197cc James) third losing 131 marks. S.R. Wardell (500cc Norton) was fourth. There were 17 entries.

The following month, on Sunday 14th March, Bernard rode for the Boston Club and won the Lincoln Trophy trial held in the Ironstone quarries at Greetwell. There were 24 competitors, with Bernard (197cc James) the winner having lost only 14 marks. The other results were:

2nd and first-class award M. Frith (197cc James)
3rd and first-class award T. Organ (197cc James)
4th and second-class award R. Lingard (197cc James)
5th and second-class award J. Sodergren (500cc Norton)

Other local riders that won awards were:
10th G. Periam Jnr (197cc James)
13th A.E Codd (Bernard's brother) (350cc Matchless)

On 28th April, 1954, Bernard entered the National Bemrose Trophy Trial, a trade-supported event held in the Peak District. There were 150 solo entries, including A.E. Codd and M. Frith from Hagworthingham. This is recorded as Bernard's first major event. The winner was J.V. Smith, the BSA works rider, who lost just 10 marks. Bernard was riding his 197cc James and completed the 56-mile rocky course with a loss of 65 marks; M. Frith lost the same number of marks, also on a James. A.E. Wildman from Spilsby retired. Bernard put up the best performance by a Grimsby club rider, thereby winning the Grimsby Club award.

Bernard rode in the tough East Midlands Trial in Derbyshire on 14th November 1954. He lost 58 marks and won a second-class award, missing out on a first-class award by only one mark. The trial started at Hartington and included many of the hazards used in the national events. The winner was N.H. Storer on a James, losing just 20 marks. Bill Lomas, the Royal Enfield factory rider, won the 500cc event.

In February 1955 Bernard won the Premier award at the Peterborough Club Trial. This was the Millfield Cup sporting trial, and he lost 50 marks riding his 197cc James. First class awards went to:

D. Bowerman (Matchless) losing 51 marks
M. Frith (James) losing 69 marks
G. Periam (James) losing 77 marks
C.L. Watkins (James) losing 86 marks

In April 1955 Bernard won the Fred Tomblin Memorial Trophy at the Banovallum MCC sporting trial held on a course starting near Hagworthingham. The result was:

B.D. Codd (197cc James) lost 20 marks
R. Lingard (197cc James) lost 46 marks
M. Frith (197cc James) lost 46 marks

R. Lingard, from Wragby, was awarded second place because he travelled furthest with least loss of marks.

CHAPTER TWO

ROAD RACING

"There's a star in the making"

Thoughts soon turned to Road Racing: *"I had always wanted to race, and I sought Austin's advice on a suitable machine,"* Bernard said. Austin discussed this with Sam Coupland and, as a result, they decided to take Bernard under their wing as they had done with Dickie Dale. This was in the Spring of 1955 and the machine they thought most suitable was a 350cc BSA Goldstar. Austin bought the bike (as he had done with Bernard's previous mounts), and Sam Coupland modified and tuned the BSA as he had done for Austin back in his racing days. In the six meetings Bernard competed in during the 1955 season he failed to win any races, but he did have some promising results. He competed at Snetterton, Cadwell Park, and Brough.

The first of these was Snetterton on Sunday 31st July, followed by Cadwell Park the next day, Bank Holiday Monday. Unlike today, where riders transport their machines and equipment to and from race meetings in luxurious transporters, Bernard took his BSA to that first meeting at Snetterton in a pig trailer.

Bernard didn't feature in the results for the meeting at Snetterton, which isn't surprising as it was his first venture at Road Racing. The results were:

Ultra-lightweight 125cc
1st J. Hogan (MV Agusta) 66.60mph
2nd R.W. Porter (MV Agusta)
3rd F.H. Burman (EMC Puch)

Lightweight 175cc -250cc
1st J. Surtees (NSU) 78.96mph
2nd J. Eckart (Excelsior)
3rd F.H. Burman (EMC Puch)

Junior 350cc Solo
1st J. Surtees (Norton) 82.03mph

2nd M.P. O'Rouke (AJS)
3rd F.M. Fox (Norton)

500cc Solo
1st J. Surtees (Norton) 84.54mph
2nd M.P. O'Rouke (AJS)
3rd G. Tanner (Norton)

500cc Sidecar
1st J. Beeton (Norton Watsonian) 75.84mph
2nd F. Taylor (Norton)
3rd L.W. Taylor (Norton Watsonian)

1200cc Sidecar
1st F. Taylor (500cc Norton) 76.30mph
2nd Bill Boddice (Norton Watsonian)
3rd L.W. Taylor (Norton Watsonian)

Sidecar Handicap
1st J.F. Swindells (Norton) 66.77mph
2nd P. Millard (Norton)
3rd E. Walker (Norton)

The following day at Cadwell Park, Bernard was again entered into the event by Austin Munks, possibly again transporting his BSA in the pig trailer.

His first race was event two in the programme, the Junior race for solo machines under 350cc. This was run over three heats, with the first five in each heat qualifying for the final. Each heat was run over six laps. The result of the first heat, scheduled to start at 12.35pm was:

1st D.A. Tutty (348cc Norton) 7m 59.2sec
2nd A. Evans (348cc Norton) 8m 2.4sec
3rd G.H. Brooks (348cc Norton) 8m 2.8sec
4th J.C. Smith (348cc AJS) 8m 27.4sec
5th D.H. Nourish (348cc AJS) 8m 27.6sec

The result of heat two, scheduled to start at 1.40pm was:

1st J. Eckart (348cc Norton) 7m 53.6sec
2nd K.H. Patrick (348cc BSA) 7m 53.8sec
3rd P. Ferbrache (348cc BSA) 7m 57sec
4th G. Monty (348cc GMS) 8m 10.4sec
5th A. Newstead (348cc AJS) 8m 10.6sec

Bernard was in heat three, scheduled to start at 2.00pm, with the race number 64. The race was dominated by George Catlin from Wragby (348cc Norton) who led from start to finish. He was followed by H. Plews (349cc AJS) for the first four laps until he was passed by S.T. Barnett (348cc Norton) who then followed Catlin home to finish second. Bernard was running in third place for the first three laps but then dropped down to fifth until the final lap, when he passed H. Plews to regain fourth place and qualify for the final. H. Plews also qualified for the final with a fifth-place finish. No race times were found for this heat.

The Junior event final was scheduled to start at 3.15pm and run over eight laps. Peter Ferbrache (348cc BSA) led at the start followed by J. Eckert (348cc Norton); on lap two the positions were reversed, and J. Eckert then led for the remainder of the race and took the win. G. Catlin (348cc Norton) passed Peter Ferbrache on lap five and held second place to the end of the race. Ferbrache finished third, with K.H. Patrick (348cc BSA) finishing fourth. F. Wallis (348cc BSA) was fifth and D.A. Tutty (348cc Norton) sixth. Bernard was in tenth place for the first two laps before being overtaken by S.T. Barnett (348cc Norton) on lap three; he regained tenth place for laps four and five only to be passed by G.H. Brooks (348cc Norton) on lap six which demoted him to eleventh place where he finished. The results were:

1st J. Eckert (348cc Norton) 10m 16.4sec £20.00
2nd G. Catlin (348cc Norton) 10m 17.8sec £14.00
3rd P. Ferbrache (348cc BSA) 10m 27sec £7.00
4th K.H. Patrick (348cc BSA) 10m 27.8sec £5.00
5th F. Wallis (348cc BSA) 10m 28.6sec £3.00
6th D.A. Tutty (348cc Norton) 10m 28.8sec £2.00

Event five, scheduled to start at 4.05pm, was the senior (Folbigg Trophy) race for machines up to 1000cc. Again, there were three heats run over six laps with the first five from each heat qualifying for the 12-lap final. H. Plews (499cc Norton) led heat one from start to finish with G. Catlin (499cc Norton) second and J. Walker (498cc SCS) third; W.R. Smith (498cc Triumph) was fourth for the first three laps but was then passed by P. Ferbrache (499cc Norton) mid-race. Ferbrache finished fourth, 3.8sec ahead of Smith in fifth. The result of heat one was:

1st H. Plews (499cc Norton) 7m 44.8sec
2nd G. Catlin (499cc Norton) 7m 45.4sec
3rd J. Walker (498cc SCS) 7m 52.2sec
4th P. Ferbrache (499cc Norton) 7m 57.8sec
5th W.R. Smith (498cc Triumph) 8m 1.6sec

Heat two, scheduled to start at 4.55pm, was won by J.B. Denton (499cc Norton) who led from start to finish. A. Evans (499cc Norton) was second, J. Eckert (499cc Norton) was third with N.G. Chalkley (998cc Vincent) fourth and P.E.S. Webb (499cc JABS) finishing fifth.

1st J.B. Denton (499cc Norton) 7m 50.6sec
2nd A. Evans (499cc Norton) 7m 54.4sec
3rd J. Eckert (499cc Norton 7m 56.4sec
4th N.G. Chalkley (998cc Vincent) 7m 57.2sec
5th P.E.S. Webb (499cc JABS) 8m 1sec

Heat three was scheduled to start at 5.15pm and in the programme Bernard was listed in the reserves but, with J.H.T. Harris (499cc Matchless) not being able to compete, he got his chance. J.P. Hodgkin (499cc Vincent) won the race, taking the lead with two laps to go from F. Wallis (499cc BSA) who finished second. Third was S.T. Barnett (499cc Norton) and fourth was K.H. Patrick (348cc BSA). Bernard (348cc BSA) came fifth. He must have had a terrible start as he is not mentioned in the top fifteen riders until lap three when he appears in fifth place, and he holds that position until the end thereby qualifying for the final. The result of heat three was:

1st J.P. Hodgkin (499cc Vincent) 7m 45sec
2nd F. Wallis (499cc BSA) 7m 46.4sec
3rd S.T. Barnett (499cc Norton) 7m 48.8sec
4th K.H. Patrick (348cc BSA) 7m 53sec
5th B.D. Codd (348cc BSA) 7m 58.2sec
6th E.B. Jones (499cc Norton) 7m 58.4sec

The final of the Senior solo Folbigg Trophy was scheduled to start at 6.05pm and run over twelve laps. J.P. Hodgkin (499cc Vincent) took the lead on lap one and won by over 15 seconds, J.B. Denton was second after passing H. Plews (499cc Norton) on lap five, H. Plews finished third, F. Wallis (499cc BSA) was fourth and A. Evans (499cc Norton) finished fifth. The result of the final was:

1st J.P. Hodgkin (499cc Vincent) 15m 1sec £25.00
2nd J.B. Denton (499cc Norton) 15m 16.4sec £18.00
3rd H. Plews (499cc Norton) 15m 20sec £12.00
4th F. Wallis (499cc BSA) 15m 22.6sec £9.00
5th A. Evans (499cc Norton) 15m 27.4sec £6.00
6th S.T. Barnett (499cc Norton) 15m 29sec £4.00

Bernard's race was quite eventful but not lucrative: on his first lap he was thirteenth, on laps two and three he moved down to fourteenth before moving back up one place to thirteenth for laps four and five; on lap six he was twelfth, on laps seven, eight and nine he progressed to eleventh and on lap ten he moved up to tenth place, which is the position in which he crossed the finish line. Considering the event was for machines up to 1000cc Bernard was the highest placed 348cc rider and, it being his first weekend road racing, I don't think that was a bad result.

September 10th was the date of the next meeting at the 2.7-mile Snetterton circuit in Norfolk, where Bernard didn't feature in the results or reports. The Class winners were:

125cc J. Hogan (MV Agusta) 68.79mph
250cc J. Surtees (NSU) 77.49mph
350cc R. McIntyre (Norton) 81.12mph
500cc J. Surtees (Norton) 85.54mph
500cc Sidecar P.V. Harris (Norton) 79.28mph
1200cc Sidecar P.V. Harris (500cc Norton) 79.33mph
Vintage W.A Wiffen (500cc Rudge) 72mph

John Surtees won the Lightweight and Senior championship events at Cadwell Park on the following day, 11th September 1955, riding the NSU in the lightweight, and the latest works Norton in the Senior. In doing so he broke the eight-lap record for the one-and-a-quarter mile circuit. He was unable to compete in the Junior event because of the damage to his 348cc machine from the previous day at Snetterton, which enabled George Catlin from Minting in Lincolnshire to win the event despite coming up against some quality riders.

In the third heat of the 350cc championship event Bernard was slow to get away on his BSA Goldstar but still managed to finish sixth, despite strong competition from riders such as G. Catlin, D.A. Tutty, J. Eckert, K.H. Patrick, and John Hartle (a works Norton rider). Bernard's time was just six-tenths of a second slower than the winner of the previous heat. G. Catlin (348cc Norton) led the race from start to finish, J. Hartle (348cc Norton) finished second and J. Eckert (349cc Norton) third. G. Catlin won the final of the 350cc Championship with a nine-second margin over second-placed Fred Wallis (348cc AJS) and P.H. Taite (348cc AJS) third. J. Hartle (348cc Norton) crashed at Coppice Corner on lap five while in sixth place.

350cc solo championship Final (12 laps)

1st G. Catlin (499cc Norton) 16m 40.2sec, 53.6mph £25.00
2nd F. Wallis (348cc AJS) £20.00
3rd P.H. Taite (348cc AJS) £15.00
4TH J. Eckert (349cc Norton) £8.00

The final of the sidecar "scratch" competition saw a strong turn-out, including Jack Beeton (499cc Norton / Watsonian), Bill Bodice (499cc Norton), F. Hanks (498cc Matchless), Pip Harris (498cc Norton), Frank Taylor (499cc Norton), Cyril Smith (former world champion) (499cc Norton/ Watsonian), Australian Bob Mitchell (499cc Norton) and R. Beedham (499cc Norton) with his lady passenger, Miss Y. Johnson.

Harris led at the start followed by Taylor, Beeton, and Mitchell. These placings remained unchanged until lap four, when Beeton passed Taylor at Coppice Corner. Mitchell followed as they thundered along the top straight. Harris won by seven seconds from Beeton.

Sidecar Championship Final (8 laps)

1st P.V. Harris / R. Campbell (498cc Norton) 10m 45.6sec, 55.2mph £30.00
2nd J. Beeton / C. Billingham (499cc Norton) £20.00
3rd R. Mitchell / M. George (499cc Norton) £12.00
4th F. Taylor / A. Johnson (499cc Norton) £6.00

Lightweight championship Final (8 laps)
For solo machines under 250cc
1st J. Surtees (248cc NSU) 11m 28sec, 52.3mph £12.00
2nd J.R. Simpson (248cc Velocette) £8.00
3rd J. Eckert (249cc Excelsior) £5.00
4th J. Patrick (248cc Velocette) £5.00

J.P. Hodgkin (499cc Vincent) got a good start in the Senior Championship Final but by the time they had reached the Mountain, J. Surtees (499cc Norton) had taken the lead. G. Catlin (499cc Norton), H. Plews (499cc Norton) Fred Wallis (499cc BSA), J. Hartle (499cc Norton), and A. Evans (499cc Norton) had closed in on Hodgkin by lap four.

Bernard rode his BSA Goldstar to a creditable twelfth place and the commentator, Murry Walker, remarked *"There's a star in the making."* Surtees kept extending his lead with each lap and crossed the line with a 24.6sec lead. This broke the eight-lap record - which had been set in 1954 by Brian Freestone of Lincoln - by 2.2sec. The result of the Final was:

Senior Championship Final (12 laps)
1st J. Surtees (499cc Norton) 14m 39.8sec, 61.5mph £40.00
2nd P. Hodgkin (499cc Vincent) £30.00
3rd J. Hartle (499cc Norton) £20.00
4th P.H. Taite (498cc Norton) £10.00

Bernard was listed in the programme as third reserve in heat three for this event, but I can't find any mention of him in any of the race reports or results, so I assume he didn't get the opportunity to race.

Sidecar Handicap race (8 laps)
1st E. Walker / D.G. Roberts (499cc W.R. Norton) 11m 2sec, 53.7mph £20.00
2nd W.G. Boddice / W. Storr (499cc Norton) £12.00
3rd R. Mitchell / M. George (499cc Norton) £7.00
4th F. Hanks / E. Dorman (498cc Matchless) £4.00

500cc Final (8 laps)
For solo machines under 500cc
1st J. Hartle (499cc Norton) 10m 00sec, 60mph £25.00

2nd G. Catlin (499cc Norton) £20.00
3rd B. Freeston (499cc Norton) 15.00
4th F. Wallis (499cc BSA) £10.00

Bernard was listed in the programme to compete in heat one of this event, but again there is no mention of him in any of the race reports or results. A report in The Lincolnshire Standard remarked that Bernard's BSA Goldstar was "... *almost certainly an improved model in some respects"*; obviously a compliment to the technical ability of Sam Coupland who did the tuning on Bernard's machines.

John Surtees - the king of short circuits - again dominated the Road Race meeting at Brough Aerodrome on September 25th, a 1.2-mile-long circuit situated in the East Riding of Yorkshire on the perimeter road of the Second World War airfield. Surtees won all three solo classes with ease and broke the existing lap record in each event. There were over 120 solo competitors and more than 20 entries in the sidecar class. Ex-world champion, Cyril Smith, was the top rider in the sidecar events but had to retire in the sidecar scratch final while leading with a broken exhaust pipe.

B. Mitchell, who was a substitute entry taking the place of P.V. Harris, won the sidecar scratch race but had to be content with second place in the Handicap final behind A.A. Lang. Cyril Smith broke the handicap sidecar lap record of 61.04mph with a new speed of 61.94mph while trying to catch the leaders, but could only finish fifth. Bernard finished second in heat three of the 350cc event behind John Surtees, and sixth in the final.

250cc
1st J. Surtees (NSU) Fastest lap 62.31mph
2nd J.R. Simpson (Velocette)
3rd D. Whelan (Velocette)

350cc
1st J. Surtees (Norton) Fastest lap 65.40mph
2nd R. McIntyre (Norton)
3rd F.M. Fox (Norton)
4th A. King (BSA)
5th K.H. Patrick (BSA)
6th B.D. Codd (BSA)

500cc
1st J. Surtees (Norton) Fastest lap 66.02mph
2nd F.M Fox (Norton)
3rd J.A. Storr (Norton)

1000cc
J. Surtees (500cc Norton) Fastest lap 64.69mph

1200cc Sidecars
1st R. Mitchell (500cc Norton)
2nd B. Boddice (Norton)
3rd J. Beeton (Norton)
Fastest lap Cyril Smith 60.80mph

Sidecar Handicap
1st A.A. Lang (Norton)
2nd B. Mitchell (Norton)
3rd C. Freeman (Norton)
Fastest lap Cyril Smith 61.94mph

On Sunday 2nd October Bernard had his best result so far at Cadwell Park, finishing third, and only four machine lengths behind D.A. Tutty (348cc Norton) in the 350cc solo race. The results were:

1st J. Hartle (348cc Norton) 10m 1sec, 59.95mph, a new record for eight laps
2nd D.A. Tutty (348cc Norton)
3rd B.D. Codd (348cc BSA)
4th K.H. Patrick (348cc BSA)

In the 1000cc race, Peter Ferbrache (499cc Norton) led into the Mountain on the first lap followed by G. Catlin (499cc Norton), F. Wallis (499cc BSA), W.R. Smith (498cc Triumph), A. Evans (499cc Norton), J. Walker (SCS), B. Freestone (Norton), Alastair King (Norton), and last but one after a poor start Bernard, riding the only 350cc machine in the race. G. Catlin and F. Wallis were wheel-to-wheel going into Coppice Corner making it difficult for P. Ferbrache to hold them back, and King moved into third place on lap five. Bernard moved up to eighth place, overtaking six 500cc riders. On lap six, King led from Catlin, Wallis and Ferbrache. Under pressure, King lost control of his Norton at the hairpin bringing down Catlin and Wallis. Ferbrache inherited the lead and crossed the line for an unexpected win, and J.B. Denton (499cc Norton) was second. Wallis must have re-joined the race as it reports he finished third, B. Freestone fourth, A. Evans fifth, and Bernard sixth. The result was:

1000cc Solo Final
1st P. Ferbrache (499cc Norton) 10m 9.8sec, 59.1mph
2nd J.B. Denton (499cc Norton)
3rd F. Wallis (499cc BSA)
4th B. Freestone (499cc Norton)
5th A. Evans (499cc Norton)
6th B.D. Codd (348cc BSA)

Wilf Spence (499cc Norton) of Alford, receiving a 70-second advantage over the backmarker "Pip" Harris" (499cc Norton), was first away in the Sidecar Handicap race, and not until the last lap did he look like being caught. With a lap to go Harris was still nine seconds behind Spence as they entered the woodland section but, as they exited Barn Corner, Harris was right on the back of Spence with just the run to the finish line left. Spence held on for the win, with Harris coasting over the line with his chain coming off in the last few yards. The result was:

Sidecar Handicap Race
1st W. Spence (499cc Norton) 11m 30.4sec, 51.5mph
2nd P.V. Harris (499cc Norton)
3rd J. Beeton (499cc Norton)
4th F. Hanks (498cc Matchless)

Sidecar Scratch Race Final
1st P.V Harris (499cc Norton) 10m 23sec, 57.7mph
2nd R. Mitchell (499cc Norton)
3rd F. Hanks (499cc Matchless)
4th F. Taylor (499cc Norton)

With the conclusion of the Road Racing season Bernard kept his hand in with Trials competitions. One such event was The Lincolnshire Group Motorcycle Team Trial, held in the Binbrook area on Sunday 20th November 1955. Bernard won the "Harvey Gill Cup" for best individual rider, losing 29 marks, three less than A.L. Webb the Lincoln rider. The other results were:

2nd A.L. Webb 32 marks
3rd G.A. Fowler 33 marks
4th M. Little 34 marks

In the club event, teams were entered by Horncastle (Banovallum), Grimsby, Scunthorpe, Gainsborough, Lincoln, North Lincs, and Owston Ferry. Best team performance was achieved by Grimsby (A) with a loss of 115 marks, a lead of 3 marks over Banovallum.

Starting and finishing at Binbrook, the course of approximately 20 miles included 20 observed sections with varying levels of severity. The course was covered twice. The results for the team events were:

1st Grimsby (A): M. Little, D. Robinson, G.A. Fowler, 115 marks
2nd Banovallum: B.D. Codd, F. Lingard, K.R. Craggs, 118 marks
3rd Lincoln: A.L Webb, K. Russell, K. Barnard, 137 marks

Bernard was unable to attend the Banovallum MCC Dinner in December, held at The Golf Hotel in Woodhall Spa, Lincolnshire, as he was taking part in 15 days training with the RAF. His father, Mr D.H. Codd, was there to receive Bernard's trophy, which was presented to him by Bill Boddice the sidecar racer.

There are two more reports I found in the scrapbook compiled by Bernard's mother, which concern a 'Cart Track' Trial that Bernard participated in driving an Austin A90, and a 'Night Trial'. Unfortunately, there is no date attached to the newspaper cuttings but I'm sure they date from some point in 1956 as it refers to Bernard as *"a rising motorcycle road-racer"*.

The Boston & District Motorcycle and Light Car Club's Semi-Sporting Trial started at the Red Cow public house at Bargate End, Boston. There were 14 competitors, and each was given a set of map references for the corresponding checkpoints, along with a list of standard times to arrive at these points. The competitors own time was calculated by adding his number in minutes to the standard time. The first check was situated just off the A17 Main Road near Heckington, relatively easy to find in the time allotted. The second check point was in a muddy farmyard at Little Hale Fen, which some found more difficult, and many were reduced to walking pace and therefore points were lost. The first unmanned checkpoint was at Welby, near Grantham, and was marked by a yellow rectangle on a small post. After this it was on to the furthest checkpoint at Stapleford Woods near Newark. On arriving at the penultimate check point on the outskirts of Lincoln, a route card was used to reach the manoeuvrability tests at Metheringham Aerodrome, and the end of the trial. Penalties were given for missing a checkpoint, approaching a checkpoint from the wrong direction, failing to close a gate and - of course - time penalties.

Bernard won the Trial losing just 64 points, 20 on the road section and 44 in the special tests where it was said that his A90 must have taken more handling than the smaller cars in the event.

1st B.D. Codd (Austin A90) lost 64 points
2nd J. Morton (Austin 8) lost 87 points
3rd A.E. Codd (Morris Minor) lost 199 points
4th R. Marriott (Ford Anglia) lost 246 points
5th G.R. Brown (Austin A 40) lost 357 points
6th G.F. Harley (Austin A30) lost 589 points
7th M. Belton (Ford Prefect) lost 670 points
8th T.W. Roberts (Vauxhall) lost 784 points
9th H. Bainbridge (Panther sidecar) lost 1026 points
10th B. White (Austin 7) lost 1184 points
11th M.J. Frank (197cc James) lost 1236 points

J. Morton who finished second was initially recorded as losing 387 points because he was penalised 300 points for taking a different route to one of the checkpoints, but when it was reviewed it showed that the road he should have taken was not shown on his map.

The second report was also organised by the Boston & District Motorcycle & Light Car Club and refers to a night Trial held on a Saturday evening, which again started from the Red Cow, Boston. There were 26 starters for the trial, but it turned out to be so difficult only 18 made it back to the Red Cow.

The competitors were given a route card with directions and road numbers, which should have enabled them to navigate their way to Heckington via Kirton-Holme, Swineshead and East Heckington. After completing the first section there was an Anti-Dazzle test conducted in a lay-by near Heckington on the A17. Only six competitors lost marks at this test. There were just four checkpoints on the route: East Heckington, Millthorpe crossroads, Quadring Church (which most competitors failed to locate) and Frampton Church. The route back to the Red Cow included Dunsby, Gosberton Risegate, Quadring, Wigtoft, Kirton and Frampton, a total distance of 51 miles.

All the motorcycles in the trial failed to finish and included entries from Banovallum Motorcycle Club (Horncastle) and Skegness Motor Club.

1st J.D. Pett (Austin) lost 30 marks
2nd R. Holmes (Singer) lost 32 marks
3rd G. Marriott (Ford Anglia) lost 33 marks
4th J. Shooter (Standard 8) lost 37 marks
5th C. Ellis (Ford Anglia) lost 40 marks
6th A. Codd (Morris) lost 43 marks
7th J. Chapman (Morris) lost 47 marks
8th D. Addy (Lea Francis) lost 59 marks
9th R.F. Knowles (Hillman) lost 65 marks
10th = B. White (Austin 7) lost 69 marks
N.H Lakin (Austin) lost 69 marks
G.W. Baker (Morris) lost 69 marks
G.R. Brown (Austin) lost 69 marks
14th B. Codd (Austin A90) lost 79 marks
15th = K.C. Roe (Volkswagen) lost 80 marks
P. Fountain (Morris) lost 80 marks
17th G.R. Allewell (Morris) lost 84 marks
18th R. Parker (MG) lost 114 marks

CHAPTER THREE

A BRIEF HISTORY OF CADWELL PARK

"Mini Nürburgring"

The Cadwell Park circuit of today is acknowledged by many motor sport enthusiasts to be one of the most exciting (and certainly one of the most picturesque) racetracks in the country. Situated in the Lincolnshire Wolds between the quaint market towns of Louth and Horncastle, this undulating circuit is not just a favourite for motorcycle events but hosts car and go-kart meetings as well.

Cadwell's story begins in 1926 when the land was purchased by Mansfield Wilkinson for the purpose of shooting game. Mansfield's son, Charles - at this time an auctioneer and estate agent working in Louth - had other plans for the land. He could see it as a potential site for a motorcycle racing circuit. After some time, he persuaded his father to allow him to set out a rough track centred round the Old Manor House. This was three-quarters of a mile in length and had a very rough, uneven surface of broken chalk which would have been very dusty in dry conditions and very sticky in the wet.

The first race meeting was held on Sunday 24th June 1934 and in those early days the sidecars would race in a clockwise direction, but the solos would race anti-clockwise, meaning the solos would go down the mountain section instead of up as they do today. What the reasoning behind this was I don't know.

The racing proved to be very successful, and popular with not just local Lincolnshire racing fans but enthusiastic fans from across the country. By May 1935 the track had been resurfaced but was still very loose and dusty and was challenging for the competitors. More track improvements were made in 1937, which attracted more competitors, and speeds and times increased. Cadwell was now considered to be one of the leading race circuits in the country. An extension to the concrete section of the track costing £500 was completed in time for the Whit Monday meeting in 1938.

The circuit was extended to a mile-and-a-quarter in length for the start of the 1953 season meaning a longer main straight leading to Coppice Hill, which then took you to the 90° righthand bend called Mansfield which, in turn, led to the new lefthand bend at the bottom of the Mountain. This Mountain section of the circuit was a popular spectator point and as exciting in those early days as it is today.

The new two-and-a-quarter-mile-long circuit that we know today - nicknamed by some as the mini-Nürburgring - was first used at the August Bank Holiday Monday meeting in 1961. These improvements turned Coppice Corner (the first corner after the start line) into the fastest corner on the circuit and led to the new long sweeping righthand bend called Charlies. This is followed by Park Straight, which takes you to the highest part of the circuit and the 90° righthand Park Corner followed by the righthand bend which was first called Donington Curve but has since been renamed Chris Curve, then to the Gooseneck followed by the fast downhill section and the now lefthand bend called Mansfield and then on to the Mountain section. In later years, a chicane was added between Mansfield and the Mountain section to reduce speeds as the machines got faster. After cresting the Mountain there is a short run past the paddock area to Hall Bends, which is a series of right-and lefthand bends that lead to the slowest part of the circuit, the righthand Hairpin Corner; there is then a short straight to Barn Corner that then runs downhill to the finish line.

Cadwell Park would be the venue for international events in the 1960s and 70s, attracting the superstars of the day such as Mike Hailwood, Giacomo Agostini, Bill Ivy, Phil Read, Barry Sheene and many more. The circuit today is owned and maintained by MSV (Motorsport Vision), a business associated with former racing driver Jonathon Palmer, and hosts a round of BSB (British Superbike) series.

Bernard with his
350cc AJS that he
got for his 16th birthday

Bernard in
unknown Trials event

Bernard competing
in 'The Bemrose
Trophy Trial March 1954'

WIN FOR WRANGLE RIDER

Difficult Banovallum trial

WRANGLE trials star, Bernard Codd scored another success on Sunday when he won the Horncastle (Banovallum) Motor Cycle Club's George Frith Challenge Cup trial, held at Winceby.

Riding Austin Munks' 197 c.c. James, he completed the difficult course with a loss of 35 marks.

Just two marks behind, was M. Frith, of Hagworthingham, son of the donor of the Cup who, temporarily without a trials model of his own "shared" a James with another competitor.

Twisting climbs and descents among the rabbit ho'es formed the majority of the sections but there were two "mud and water" hazards in the valley bottom which proved real stoppers.

On these two both Codd and Frith each lost a total of 21.

Codd was troubled by a blocked petrol pipe on the first lap which cost him five marks when the engine died half-way through a section

CLOSE FINISH

There was a tie for third place between L. Watkin (Grantham) James, and R. Lingard (Horncastle) James, who lost 50 marks. G. Periam (Boston) also James-mounted was fifth with 51 marks lost. There were 17 competitors.

Results: 1, B. D. Codd, 35 marks lost. 2, M. Frith, 37; 3, L. Watkin and R Lingard 50; 5, G. Periam, 51. 6, D. Allen, 54; 7, T. Organ, 64; 8, A.W. Bishop 66; 9, D. Halker, 69; 10 J. Murray, 85.

MOTOR CYCLING

BERNARD CODD, of Wrangle, a member of the Boston Club, won the Lincoln Trophy Trial held in the ironstone quarries, Greetwell, on Sunday, results of which were released yesterday.

He was riding a 197 c.c. James, and lost only 14 marks.

Other results were:—2nd and first-class award, M. Frith (197 James), Horncastle; 3rd and first-class award, T. Organ (197 James), Lincoln; 4th and second-class award, R. Lingard (197 James), Wragby; 5th and second-class award, J. Sodergren (500 c.c. Norton), Grimsby; 10th, G. Periam, junior (197 James); 13th, A. E. Codd (350 Matchless). There were 24 competitors.

WON NEWARK TRIAL

Bernard Codd, of Wrangle, riding a 197 c.c. James, won the Hole's Cup trial organised by the Newark M.C.C. on Sunday. He lost only 11 marks. Second was Reg Lingard (197 James), of Wragby, lost 25, and third Johnny Duncan, of Newark (197 c.c. Sun) lost 34 marks.

BERNARD CODD, of Wrangle, made a good start to the trials season on Saturday, when he competed in a Grimsby Club event.

Riding Austin Munk's 500 c.c. Norton, he lost only 13 marks to win the premier award, the "Wardell" trophy. Second man, Wardell, lost 15 marks, and the third, Gartside, lost 20. Codd completes his National Service in the R.A.F. next month, and hopes to compete in some of the bigger sporting trials this winter.

Trials results, unfortunately undated (taken from Mrs Codd's scrapbook)

* * *

Bernard Codd, the Wrangle motor-cyclist won the Grimsby Club's B.S.A. Cup sporting trial for the fourth year in succession last week-end. The previous week he won the Grantham Club's Trial, riding a 197 c.c. James' on both occasions.

* * *

MOTOR CYCLING

There was a disappointingly small entry for the Banovallum Motor Cycle Club's sporting trial held over a course starting near Hagworthingham on Sunday.

Winner of the Fred Tomblin Memorial Trophy was Bernard Codd, of Wrangle, riding a 197 c.c. James, who lost 20 marks; 2nd, R. Lingard (Wragby) 197 c.c. James, 46 marks; 3rd, M. Frith (Hagworthingham) 197 c.c. James. 46 marks. Lingard takes second place award because he travelled furthest with least loss of marks.

Bannovallum Main Road Trial results: Cars, J. C. Strawson (Riley). Motor-cycles, G. H. Suddaby (B.S.A.).

Ross Porter of Spalding, who has a new 125 c.c. M.V. Agusta crashed at Cascades corner when leading a field of 34 riders at Oulton Park recently. Happily he escaped with cuts and abrasions. He finished second at Brands Hatch recently.

Reference to Dickie Dale's fine achievements and a photograph appear on another page.

Jack Beeton of Louth will be competing in motor sidecar events at Silverstone to-morrow (Saturday).

* * *

Bernard Codd, of Wrangle, scored his third successive motor cycle trials win on Sunday when he won the Peterborough Club's event.

* * *

MOTOR-CYCLING

LINCS. TEAM TRIAL

Wrangle rider best individual

B. D. Codd, of Wrangle, was the individual winner of the Lincolnshire Group motor cycle team trial held in the Binbrook area on Sunday.

Losing 29 marks—three less than Lincoln rider A. L. Webb—he now becomes the holder of the Harvey Gill Cup.

Club teams were entered by Horncastle (Banovallum), Grimsby, Scunthorpe, Gainsborough, Lincoln, North Lincs., and Owston Ferry, the best team performance being made by Grimsby 'A', with a loss of 115 marks, a lead of three over Banovallum.

Starting and finishing at Binbrook, the course of about 20 miles including 20 observed sections of varying severity, had to be covered twice.

Results: — team, 1, Grimsby 'A' (M. Little, D. M. Robinson, G. A. Fowler) 115; 2, Banovallum (B. D. Codd, F. Lingard, K. R. Craggs) 118; 3, Lincoln, (A. L. Webb, K. Russell, K. Barnard) 137. Individual, 1, Codd (29); 2, Webb (32); 3, Fowler (33); 4, Little (34).

MOTOR CYCLING

B. D. Codd (James), of Wrangle, won the Holes Cup Trial at Newark with a loss of 23 marks; 2, A. L. Webb (James), Lincoln, 24 marks 3, K. J. Russell (Francis Barnett), Lincoln, 30.

Trials results

MOTOR-CYCLING

HORNCASTLE CLUB TRIAL

Hagworthingham Rider Wins

M. FRITH, of Hagworthingham, won the Banovallum Motor Cycle Club's first sporting trial of the year, held at Winceby on Sunday.

Riding his 197 James, he completed the long and difficult course with a loss of 98 marks.

Wrangle's Bernard Codd, on leave from the R.A.F., was third, also on a James, losing 131 marks, and his brother Arnold (Matchless) was eighth with 166. T. A. Organ (197 O.E.C.), of Lincoln, was second, four marks behind Frith, and S. R. Wardell (500 Norton), of Grimsby, was fourth.

There was an entry of 17.

The Horncastle Club's annual dance is to be held on Friday, March 7th, and on the following Sunday, the first scramble of the season will be held at Winceby. Riders already entered include Fred Wallis, Jim Burkett and Raymond Dell.

Motor Cycling

ON Saturday, the National Bemrose Trophy trial, a trade-supported event, was held in the Peak District. The 150 solo entries included the Codd brothers of Wrangle, and M. Frith, of Hagworthingham.

Competing in a major event of this type for the first time, Bernard Codd (197 James), completed the 56-mile rocky course with a loss of only 65 marks.

Frith, also James mounted, did equally well, losing the same number of marks. Arnold Codd (350 Matchless) was unlucky to lose 41 marks on time, which brought his total to 128.

Bernard Codd put up best performance by a Grimsby Club rider, and he therefore wins the Grimsby Club award. A. E. Wildman, of Spilsby, retired.

Winner was B.S.A. works rider J. V. Smith, who lost ten marks.

Trials results

MOTOR CYCLING

Wrangle motor cyclist, B. D. Codd won the Goodman Cup, premier award at a sporting trial organised by the Newark Motor Cycle and Light Car Club on Sunday.

Riding a 500 c.c. Norton, he beat D. W. Allen, of Newark, by six marks. The previous week, Codd won a Lincoln club trial, on the occasion riding a 197 c.c. James.

First six were: 1, B. D. Codd (Norton) 67 marks lost; 2, D. W. Allen (Francis Barnett) 73; 3, A. L. Webb (James) 79; 4, J. Webber (D.O.T.) 89; 5, P. W. Craven (A.J.S.) 90; 6, K. Turner (Norman) 100.

PROMISING.

Bernard Codd, of Wrangle, scored a notable success when he won the Lincoln club's recent trial at Greetwell Quarries against some very strong competition. Codd, who was riding one of Austin Munks' Nortons, is a newcomer to trials riding.

The Boston Club's film show on Tuesday at the "Peacock and Royal" Hotel was well attended, despite the weather. The 1951 World Championships and the Scottish and International Six Days Trials in colour were high-lights of the evening.

On behalf of the Club, Mr. H. A. Watson, the Chairman, wished Dicky Dale (who was among those present) success on his return to racing, and thanked the Rev. J. G. H. Cragg, Vicar of Swineshead, who operated the projector.

MOTOR-CYCLING

WRANGLE'S up - and - coming young trials rider, Bernard Codd, added another feather to his cap on Sunday, when he won the Lincoln Club's trial held at the Ironstone quarries. He lost 38 marks. He was riding a 197 c.c. James, owned by Austin Munks.

J. Sodergren and K. R. Craggs, both of Grimsby, were second and third respectively.

Bernard, who is completing National Service with the R.A.F., is stationed near Norwich, and can only ride when he gets a 48-hour leave. A week ago he was placed third in a Grimsby trial.

MOTOR CYCLING

Riding in the tough East Midlands Centre championship trial, in Derbyshire on Sunday, B. D. Codd, of Wrangle, lost 58 marks to win a second class award, missing a first class award by only one mark. The trial started at Hartington, and included many of the hazards used on national events

Winner was James rider, N. H. Storer, who lost 20 marks. Royal Enfield factory rider, Bill Lomas, won the 500 c.c. award.

TRIALS WIN.

Bernard Codd (197 James) won the Lincoln Club's Sporting Trial last Sunday with a loss of 63 marks; 2, G. Gartside (197 Sun), 89; 3, J. S. Long (490 Norton) 99

Ross Porter, of Spalding, is riding his 125 c.c. M.V. Agusta at Oulton Park, Cheshire, on Easter Monday.

BROKE RECORDS

The club's president, Mr. Dickie Dale, a rider in the Moto Guzzi team, had won seven of the world's classics, and in the past year had broken 28 world records in France.

"We make no secret of the fact," continued Mr. Belton, "that for our finances we are mainly dependent on grass track races. This year we had four really first-class meetings. We had record gates at each successive meeting, and nearly 3,000 saw our last one in October. Former national champions rode at our events, and the organisation was such that the East Midland Centre is giving us its E.M. Championships on June 24." He paid the Club's thanks to Mr. S. T. Belton for the loan of the field on which the grass races were held.

Mr. Bernard Codd had won nine out of 11 sporting trials, and a Boston team was entered in the road race championships.

B. D Codd's non-stop successes continue and the Wrangle racing and trials ace has recently won the Newark club's Gagg Trial and the Grimsby Club's Frow Trial.

Trials results

MOTOR-CYCLING

SCHOOLBOY TOP OF THE CLASS

Wrangle Rider Won 356 c.c. Award

BOSTON Grammar School pupil, and keen motor cyclist, Arnold Codd, of Wrangle, competed in the Peterborough Club's Stuffins Sporting Trial, held at Wansford on Sunday, and made best performance in the 350 c.c. class.

Riding his 350 Matchless, he did well to lose only 89 marks over a tricky course.

Arnold, who is in the Science VI, is a brother of Bernard Codd, who has won several major awards in trials throughout the county and beyond.

Until Sunday, Bernard was the holder of the Stuffins Cup, the premier award at the Peterborough trial. As he is completing National Service in the R.A.F., he was unable to compete.

Another Boston rider, G. Periam, riding a 197 James, finished sixth, losing 109 marks. There were 25 competitors.

Results: Stuffins Cup, C. L. Watkins (197 James), Grantham, 42 marks lost; best 500 c.c., F. Briggs (500 Triumph), Peterborough, 67; best 350 c.c., A. E. Codd, (350 Matchless), Wrangle, 89; best 250 c.c., K. Greer (197 D.O.T.), Peterborough, 85; best 150 c.c., M. Truetlin (150 B.S.A.), Peterborough, 223.

On Sunday the Banovollum M.C.C. will hold a sporting trial at Winceby and a strong entry is expected from Lincoln, Grimsby, Louth and Boston, in addition to the Horncastle Club's own members.

Boston motor cyclists, Bernard Codd, of Wrangle, and Austin Munks, of Leverton, had a good day on Sunday, scoring third and first places respectively in two reliability trials.

Competing in the Louth Club's Winter Shield event, Austin Munks, riding his 490 c.c. Norton, "wiped up" strong opposition from the Grimsby Club, losing three marks less than M. Little (Norton), winner of the Autumn Cup trial last month. Apart from Munks, all the other riders were from Grimsby.

The trial, which started and finished at Hubbard's Hills, Louth, covered 30 miles, and included 30 observed sections. Water-splashes were deep, but caused no retirements.

First six were: 1, A. Munks, 17 marks lost; 2, M. Little (Norton), Grimsby, lost 20; 3, J. Sodergren (Norton), Grimsby, 21; 4, K. R. Craggs (A.J.S.), Grimsby), 23; 5, H. Pickett (Norton), Grimsby, 25; and 6, S. R. Wardle (Norton), Grimsby, 26.

While Austin Munks was busy at Louth, Bernard Codd, of Wrangle, was carrying Boston's colours at the Lincoln Club's trial. Riding a 197 c.c. James, he was third to K. Frith, of Hagworthingham, on a similar machine. Winner was T. Organ, on another lightweight.

"Speed And How To Obtain It," published for "The Motor Cycle" by Iliffe and Sons, Limited, has been written primarily for the sporting motor cyclist, and secondly for the ordinary private owner who desires to obtain the highest possible performance from his machine. For both classes of enthusiast, the book gives much valuable information

From the same publishers (price 3s. 6d.) comes "The Motor Cycle Road Tests" (second series), containing performance reports, and technical data on 30 types of solo motor-cycles, sidecar outfits and scooters.

MOTOR CYCLING

B. D. Codd (James), of Wrangle, won the Holes Cup Trial at Newark with a loss of 23 marks; 2, A. L. Webb (James), Lincoln, 24 marks 3, K. J. Russell (Francis Barnett), Lincoln, 30.

Trials results

Snetterton programme
Sunday 31st July, 1955

In the paddock at Snetterton
July 1955, with
Austin Munks and the pig trailer

Cadwell Park programme
August Monday 1955

Cadwell Park programme
Sunday 11th September, 1955

In the paddock at
Cadwell Park

On track at Cadwell Park 1955

On track at Cadwell Park 1955

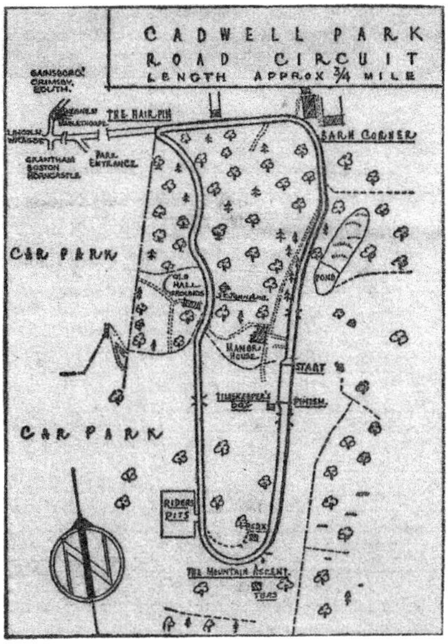

Cadwell Park lay-out 1934-1953

1953-1961

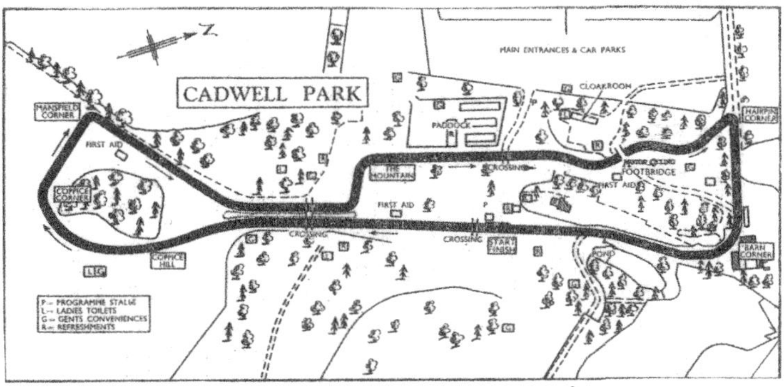

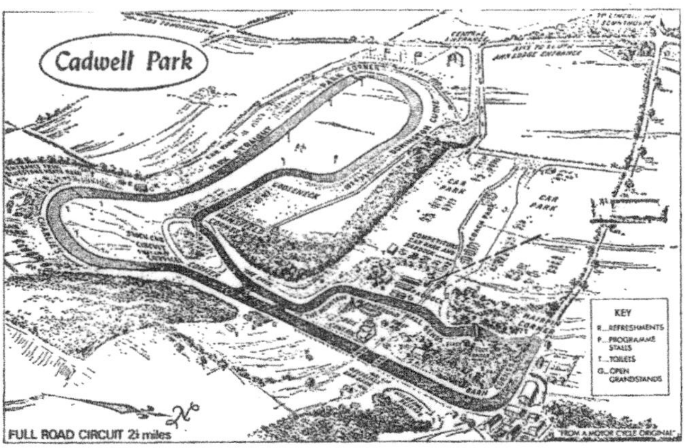

1961-present day

CHAPTER FOUR

1956

"There's only one word to describe his handling of the 500cc Norton: phenomenal"

Bernard began the year riding in trials competitions, and on January 29th he won the Peterborough Clubs trial event making this his third successive win. To add to his wins for the season Bernard entered the Lincoln's Club sporting trials held on Sunday 18th March, and the result was:

1st B.D. Codd (197cc James) 63 marks lost
2nd G. Gartside (197 Sunbeam) 89 marks lost
3rd J.S. Long (490cc Norton) 99 marks lost

For the start of the 1956 Road Racing season Austin Munks purchased an ex-John Surtees 350cc Manx Norton and a new 500cc Norton for Bernard. The first outing for these new machines was at Brough Aerodrome on 25th March. He came second to Bob McIntyre in his 350cc heat and won his 500cc heat. He finished fifth in both finals, thereby going some way to justifying the faith Austin had shown in his ability.

George Catlin finished second to Bob McIntyre in the 350cc Final riding an ex-John Surtees Streamlined Norton and was also lying in second position in the 500cc final until he collided with a straw bale at the hairpin. The class winners were:

250cc
R. McIntyre (Norton) 57.07mph

350cc
R. McIntyre (Norton) 60.72mph

Sidecar
P.V. Harris (Norton) 58.78mph

Sidecar handicap
O.E. Greenwood (Norton) 56.41mph

1000cc "Brough 25"
R. McIntyre (Norton) 63.03mph

The Easter Monday meeting at Cadwell Park on 2nd April was a thrilling spectacle for the estimated 20,000 in attendance. The close rivalry between Bernard and George Catlin, both riding Nortons and both equally determined and evenly matched was nothing short of exhilarating at times, racing just inches apart at over 100mph.

In Bernard's heat of the 350cc event he was up against George Catlin. Bernard led all the way with Catlin right behind him, and some thought that Catlin was playing a waiting game and was going to make a last corner move on Bernard at Barn Corner, but if this was the plan it didn't work, and Bernard won by half a machine's length. Jonny Walker from Frampton finished fifth on a BSA.

In the final of the 350cc event Bernard took the lead followed by G. Catlin and P. Ferbrache (Ariel JAP). On the second lap Catlin pulled out of Bernard's slipstream and just edged in front. By lap seven D. Tutty (Norton) had taken third place from Ferbrache.

As Bernard and George Catlin crossed the finish line it was so close that only the spectators standing on the line could say with any certainty who had won. It turned out to be Bernard's win. So, in two rides Bernard had achieved two wins for the Austin Munks and Sam Coupland school of motorcycling. Fred Wallis, who was still suffering from an injury he sustained in an accident he had at Brough, finished fourth. The winning time was 10m 10.6sec, which was 9.6sec outside the record set at the previous year's October meeting by J. Hartle.

In heat two of "The Folbigg Trophy" Bernard was again up against George Catlin as well as Fred Wallis and Brian Freestone. Wallis led for two laps on his Matchless Twin but was then passed by Bernard on the inside of the first bend at the bottom of the Mountain section. By lap five George Catlin was close behind Bernard and this time it was Catlin's turn to be victorious on the downhill run to the line. The winning time was 7m.40sec. Peter Ferbrache won his heat with a time just four-tenths of a second slower. Jonny Hodgkin (Vincent) was second.

In the final of "The Folbigg Trophy", run over twelve laps, Ferbrache set an early pace and at the end of lap four the order was Ferbrache, Catlin, Codd, J.B. Denton (Norton), Hodgkin and H. Plews (Norton). Jonny Walker (who had finished second in his heat on the "Stan Cooper Special") was ninth. At half distance Catlin was leading Bernard, Ferbrache, Hodgkin and Wallis, and they remained in this order for the next three laps. Bernard led exiting Barn Corner on lap ten and held on to the lead until the end, beating Catlin by just four-tenths of a second, Ferbrache was third, Hodgkin fourth and Wallis was fifth. Jonny Walker finished eighth.

Bernard crashed at the hairpin in his heat for the senior solo race, and Denton and Walker were also involved. George Catlin won the final.

The Louth Standard reported:

> *"Codd is still in his first twelve months of Road Racing and there is only one word to describe his handling of the 500cc Norton, phenomenal".*

There was a spectacular crash in the sidecar race involving Bill Beevers from Sheffield riding a new Norton and his passenger Bill Munday: a broken pipe sprayed oil onto their rear wheel, which caused their outfit to skid out of control at the S bend leading up to the woodland section of the track as they were being passed by Jack Beeton. Bill Munday was thrown through the air while Beevers was flung against the grass banking. Both men escaped with cuts and bruises. The results were:

250cc Solo Final (8 laps)
1st P. Tait (Velocette) 10m 58.4sec, 54.7mph
2nd J.F. Patrick (Velocette)
3rd T.E. Fenwick (Moto Guzzi)
4th J. Eckart (Excelsior)

350cc Final (8 laps)
1st B.D. Codd (Norton) 10m 10.6sec, 59.1mph
2nd G. Catlin (Norton)

3rd D. Tutty (Norton)
4th P. Ferbrache (Ariel- Enfield)

Folbigg Trophy Final (12 laps)
1st B.D. Codd (Norton) 14m 47.8sec, 60.85mph
2nd G. Catlin (Norton)
3rd P. Ferbrache (Norton)
4th J. Hodgkin (Vincent)

Senior solo Final (8 laps)
1st G. Catlin (Norton) 10m 34sec, 56.7mph
2nd F. Wallis (Matchless)
3rd P. Ferbrache (Norton)
4th A. Evans (499cc Norton)

500cc Sidecar Scratch Final
1st F. Hanks (Matchless) 51.7mph
2nd O.E. Greenwood (Norton)
3rd J. Beeton (Norton)
4th R.E. Cheney (Norton)

500cc Sidecar Handicap Final
1st O.E. Greenwood (Norton) 11m 41.8sec, 51.5mph
2nd F. Hanks (Matchless)
3rd J. Beeton (Norton)
4th R.E. Cheney (Norton)

The following weekend, Sunday 8th April, Bernard was at Snetterton for the meeting organised by the 'Snetterton Combined', comprising of the Motorcycle Clubs in Norfolk and Suffolk affiliated to the Eastern Centre of the ACU. He was listed in the programme as riding a 348cc BSA or 348cc Norton and a 500cc Norton. The rain that had been forecast held off but there was a strong head wind on the start and finish straight. The first event was the Ultra-Light-Weight 125cc race. M. O'Rourke (125cc MV Agusta) led the early stages of the race until mechanical failure forced him to retire and allow John Hogan (also on a 125cc MV Agusta) to take the lead and the win. Hogan's winning speed was 70.03mph, which was slower than his existing lap record of 71.37mph.

John Surtees (248cc MV Agusta) won the Lightweight 250cc event, where he built up a commanding lead over Bob McIntyre (250cc Norton). R. Mayhew (250cc Velocette) finished third after a close battle with M. O'Rourke (250cc MV Agusta) who retired on the last lap with ignition trouble and G. Ewer (250cc NSU.)

Bob McIntyre (350cc Norton) won the final of the 350cc event leading from the start. A. Trow (350cc Norton) finished second after a race-long battle with M. O'Rourke (350cc AJS). Bernard finished fourth on his 348cc Norton.

In the 500cc event there was no-one who could compete with the exceptional power of the four-cylinder 500cc MV Agusta of John Surtees. He had used a full fairing in practice but resorted to a nose fairing in the race.

The sidecar race saw Owen Greenwood (500cc Norton) finish third after a dreadful start. P.V. Harris (498cc Norton) won with Jack Beeton (499cc Norton) second. Les Nutt came out of retirement to passenger for J. Beeton as C. Billingham, his regular partner, was in hospital. The results were:

125cc Ultra-Lightweight race (4 laps)
1st J.A. Hogan (125cc MV Agusta) 9m 38sec, 67.27mph, £8.00
2nd D.H. Edlin (125cc MV Agusta) £5.00
3rd E. Pantlin (125cc LEF) £3.00
Fastest lap: J.A. Hogan (125cc MV Agusta) 2m 18.8sec, 70.03mph

250cc Light-weight race (6 laps)
1st J. Surtees (250cc MV Agusta) 12m 33.6sec, 79.77mph, £12.00
2nd R. McIntyre (250cc Norton) £10.00
3rd R. Mayhew (250cc Velocette) £8.00
Fastest lap: John Surtees (250cc MV Agusta) 2m 0.2sec, 80.86mph

350cc Junior race (10 laps)
1st R. McIntyre (350cc Norton) 19m 51sec, 81.61mph, £20.00
2nd A. Trow (350cc Norton) £12.00
3rd M. O'Rourke (350cc AJS) £8.00
4th B.D. Codd (348cc Norton) £5.00
Record lap: R. McIntyre (350cc Norton) & A. Trow (350cc Norton) 1m 57.4sec, 82.67mph
Heat Winners: R. McIntyre (350cc Norton), E. Washer (349cc AJS)

500cc Senior Final (10 laps)

1st J. Surtees (500cc MV Agusta) 18m 43.4sec, 86.52mph, £20.00
2nd R. McIntyre (500cc Norton) £12.00
3rd M. O'Rourke (500cc Norton) £8.00
4th B.J. Thompson (498cc Matchless) £5.00
Record lap: J. Surtees (500cc MV Agusta) 1m 50sec,88.37mph
Heat Winners: J. Surtees (500cc MV Agusta), R. McIntyre (500cc Norton)

500cc Sidecar race (6 laps)

1st P.V. Harris / R.M. Campbell (498cc Norton) 12m 35.4sec, 72.20mph, £15.00
2nd J. Beeton / L. Nutt (499cc Norton) £10.00
3rd O.E. Greenwood / T. Fairbrother (500cc Norton) £5.00
Fastest lap: P.V. Harris / R.M. Campbell (498cc Norton) 2m 2.4sec, 79.41mph

1200cc Sidecar race (6 laps)

1st P.V. Harris / R.M. Campbell (498cc Norton) 12m 21.6sec, 78.64mph, £15.00
2nd J. Beeton / L. Nutt (499cc Norton) £10.00
3rd O.E. Greenwood / T. Fairbrother (500cc Norton) £5.00
Fastest lap: P.V. Harris / R.M. Campbell (498cc Norton) 2m 0.4sec, 80.72mph.

Leicester Query Club organised a "tryout day" at the new 1.35-mile Kirkby Mallory track in Leicestershire on Saturday 28th April. Sixty riders turned out for this informal event. The new circuit had evolved from a previously successful grass track to a smooth new surface which promised to give the riders superb grip even in wet conditions. The day proved to be a success and several riders put up very fast times despite the short time they had to familiarise themselves with the circuit. The fastest rider of the day was Bernard with a lap time of 1m 2.2sec a speed of 78.13mph on his 499cc Norton. He achieved this time and speed despite not being able to get his machine into top gear, which was because the bike was too high geared in its set up.

W.R. Anderson was the second-quickest rider of the day, winning one of the five-lap scratch races on a 498cc Matchless. Fred Wallis - also on a 498cc Matchless - was also pleased with his performance, achieving his best lap of 77.38mph. The fastest sidecar on the day was A. Ellis (499cc Norton) with a speed of 70.84mph.

Sunday 13th May was the date of the first official meeting at Kirkby Mallory. There was a crowd of 20,000 in attendance who were blessed with fine weather and plenty of exciting racing.

Bernard won the 350cc final followed closely by E.J. Washer (AJS) and Terry Shepherd (Norton). Shepherd was the first rider to exceed an 80mph lap with a speed of 80.15mph

In the 500cc final there was an epic battle between Terry Shepherd (Norton) and George Salt (Norton), who were never threatened by any of the other riders throughout the race. Salt could pressure Shepherd but could not get past. Shepherd won with the fastest average speed of the day at 79.8mph. George Salt was second just a few yards behind and Bernard was a very creditable third with R. Jervis (Norton) fourth.

The fastest lap of the day was made by George Salt (499cc Norton) in 57.8 sec, a speed of 84.08mph. The results were:

200cc (8 laps)
1st F. Purslow (Triumph) 67.4mph
2nd E. Pantlin (L.E.S.)
3rd E. Jolly (Sunbeam)

250cc Heats (5 laps)
Heat 1
R.S. Mayhew (Velocette)

Heat 2
E.W. Tinkler (Velocette)

Heat 3
P. Minion (Velocette)

250cc Final (8 laps)
1st J. Eckart (Excelsior) 72.88mph
2nd R.S. Mayhew (Velocette)
3rd R.M. Harding (G.M.V.)

350cc Heats (5 laps)
Heat 1
J. Eckart (BSA)

Heat 2
R.H. Lilley (BSA)

Heat 3
R. Castle (BSA)

Heat 4
B.D. Codd (Norton)

Heat 5
R. Jervis (Norton)

350cc Final (8 laps)
1st B.D. Codd (Norton) 77.85mph
2nd E.J. Washer (AJS)
3rd T.S. Shepherd (Norton)

500cc Heats (5 laps)

Heat 1
T.S. Shepherd (Norton)

Heat 2
J. Eckart (Norton)

Heat 3
G.T. Salt (Norton)

Heat 4
R. Anderson (Norton)

Heat 5
R. Jervis (Norton)

500cc Final (8 laps)
1st T.S. Shepherd (Norton) 79.80mph
2nd G.T. Salt (Norton)
3rd B.D. Codd (Norton)

500cc Sidecar Heats (5 laps)

Heat 1
P.V. Harris (Norton)

Heat 2
A. Ellis (Norton)

Heat 3
C. Freeman (Norton)

Sidecar Final (8 laps)
1st P.V. Harris (Norton) 74.31mph
2nd A. Ellis (Norton)
3rd A. Young (Norton)

1000cc Sidecar Heats (5 laps)

Heat 1
O.E. Greenwood (Norton)

Heat 2
A. Ellis (Norton)

Heat 3
P.V. Harris (Norton)

Sidecar Final (8 laps)
1st A. Ellis (Norton) 74.05mph
2nd P.V. Harris (Norton
3rd A. Young (Norton)

Sidecar Handicap Final (8 laps)
1st A. Young (Norton) 72.7mph
2nd P.V. Harris (Norton)
3rd P.J. Millard (Norton)

The following weekend was the Whit Monday meeting at Cadwell Park, with an estimated 22,000 spectators attending. The meeting was sponsored by The Sheffield Telegraph.

Joint favourites George Catlin and Bernard, both on 348cc Nortons, were on the front row for the 350cc final. Catlin fired his Norton up straightaway and led going up Coppice Hill while Bernard was still pushing his Norton and was last away. By the end of lap two Bernard had passed ten riders to reach fourth place, and by the next lap he was in second place having passed W.H. Hocking (348cc Norton) and then Phil Tait (348cc Velocette). On the exit of Barn Corner on the last lap Bernard was followed by J.A. Sugden (348cc BSA) on his first Cadwell Park appearance; third was K.H. Patrick (348cc BSA) and fourth was Brian Freestone (348cc Norton). George Catlin coasted in next in fifth position with a petrol-starved engine. Bernard crossed the line to win with Patrick second, Freestone third and Sugden fourth.

In the first heat of the sidecar scratch race O.E. Greenwood, while lying second and chasing "Pip" Harris, turned his Norton Streamliner over in the woodland section of the course, fortunately without serious injury. John Harris ("Pip's" brother) in his first sidecar race on a 499cc Norton outfit achieved a third place, ahead of R.E. Cheney (497cc Norton).

Bernard led the twelve-lap senior "Folbigg Trophy" race on his 499cc Norton from lap two until lap seven when he had to retire with a broken petrol pipe. The results were:

Up to 250cc solo (8 laps)
1st J. Eckart (Excelsior) 10m 47.4sec
2nd P.H. Tait (Beasley Velocette)
3rd J.F. Patrick (Velocette)
Fastest lap: J. Eckart 1m 19sec

350cc solo (8 laps)
1st B.D. Codd (Norton) 10m 19.4sec
2nd K.H. Patrick (BSA)
3rd B. Freestone (BSA)
Fastest lap: B.D. Codd 1m 13.6sec

Folbigg Trophy 1000cc solo (12 laps)
1st G. Catlin (Norton) 14m 47.8sec
2nd P.A. Davey (BSA)
3RD J. Eckart (Norton)
Fastest lap: B.D. Codd 1m 11.6sec

Sidecar race (8 laps)
1st P.V. Harris (Norton) 10m 56.8sec
2nd J. Beeton (Norton)
3rd J.H.T. Harris (Norton)
Joint Fastest lap: P.V. Harris and J. Beeton 1m 20sec

Sidecar Handicap race (8 laps)
1st P.V. Harris (Norton) 11m 34.2sec
2nd B.N. Green (Norton)
3rd J.H.T. Harris (Norton)
Fastest lap: P.V. Harris 1m 15.2sec

CHAPTER FIVE

ISLE OF MAN CLUBMANS TT

"They said I could keep my winnings"

Bernard was already familiar with the Isle of Man as his parents had taken him there on holiday since he was a young boy but learning the mountain course was a different matter. As Bernard was working on the family farm, he was able to take time off to learn the circuit, but it was not going to be easy. He took his Matchless G9 road bike to the island and rode round on his own, estimating that he clocked up over a thousand miles leading up to the official practice week. Austin Munks, who had been influential in Geoff Dukes racing career, asked Duke to show Bernard round the course and give him some tips on lines for certain corners and braking points. This he did in his Aston Martin DB2. Duke told Bernard the only way to learn the course is to go round and round until it is all in your head.

Austin also took Bernard round the course, as did Dickie Dale. Under the watchful eye of these three motorcycling legends Bernard's knowledge of the circuit quickly built up and he observed where manhole covers were, shiny road surfaces, high kerbs, roadside walls, and gutters.

Austin Munks and Sam Coupland travelled over to the Island taking the two BSA Gold stars with them. Bernard had previously ridden the machines at MIRA (Motor Industry Research Association) near Nuneaton in Warwickshire, where they went on a testing day. Here they set the bikes up to Bernard's liking and Sam Coupland's high standards. Bernard recalled that the 500cc produced approximately 37 bhp at 6500rpm and the 350cc around 30 bhp at 6800rpm. This was also the first year that the Gold Star had the option of the larger 190mm front brake.

The first official practice started on the evening of Saturday 9th June at 6.30pm. The weather was perfect with the sun shining and not a cloud in the sky. Travelling marshals reported that conditions were ideal. J. Eckart (348cc BSA) was first away and at the end of the two-and-a-quarter hour session had set the fastest 350cc time of the night. The best 500cc lap time was set by

R.E. Jerrard (499cc BSA). Bernard went out on his 499cc BSA and was reported as being *"neat and notably fast"*. There were a few casualties on this first practice session: L. Chapman (499cc BSA) crashed at Quarter Bridge, sustaining only minor abrasions, but his machine was badly damaged; A. Herdman (348cc BSA) crashed at Glen Helen; A. Smith (349cc Velocette) crashed at Cruickshanks Corner and was taken to Ramsey Cottage Hospital for observation; and A.E. Culshaw (348cc BSA) suffered a broken jaw in an incident at Brandish Corner.

Fastest 500cc Lap times (1st Practice session)
1st R.E. Jerrard (BSA) 27m 41.8sec, 81.79mph
2nd D. Andrews (BSA) 28m 19.8sec, 79.94mph
3rd B.D. Codd (BSA) 28m 50sec, 78.53mph
4th P.K. Cruse (BSA) 29m 39.8sec, 76.35mph
5th W.J. Hill (BSA) 29m 54.6sec, 75.70mph
6th A.H. Jenkins (BSA) 29m 55.2sec, 75.68mph

Fastest 350cc Lap times (1st Practice session)
1st J. Eckart (BSA) 28m 51.6sec, 78.46mph
2nd D. Jervis (BSA) 29m 08.6sec, 77.70mph
3rd G.A. Borland (BSA) 30m 31.4sec, 74.19mph
4th K.W. James (BSA) 30m 35.2sec, 74.05mph
5th L.S. Rutherford (BSA) 30m 37.8sec, 73.95mph
6th J.D. Morton (BSA) 30m 43.8sec, 73.70mph

Monday morning 11th June was again perfect conditions for the second practice session, with 89 riders taking advantage of the fine dry weather. First rider away at 5.00am was D. Hagen (499cc BSA). Bernard, again out on his 499cc BSA, was reported as *"stylish"* when negotiating Signpost Corner with the ease of a rider who had ridden the Mountain Course for many years rather than someone there for the first time, and the same was said about him at the fast S-bend at Union Mills. Bernard finished this second practice session fastest overall.

Fastest 500cc Lap times (2nd Practice session)
1st B.D. Codd (BSA) 26m 40.2sec, 84.82mph
2nd R.E. Jerrard (BSA) 26m 45.8sec, 84.71mph
3rd D. Jervis (BSA) 27m 37.8sec, 82.05mph
4th F. Wallis (BSA) 27m 56.4sec, 81.06mph

5th D. Andrews (BSA) 28m 11.6sec, 80.39mph
6th P.K. Cruse (BSA) 28m 21sec, 79.88mph

Fastest 350cc lap times (2nd Practice session)
1st E. Unwin (BSA) 29m 17.4sec, 77.33mph
2nd J.D. Morton (BSA) 29m 32sec, 76.68mph
3rd A. Shepherd (Norton) 29m 52.2sec, 75.81mph
4th D. Pratt (BSA) 30m 06sec, 75.22mph
5th J.F. Righton (Velocette) 30m 06.4sec, 75.22mph
6th D.H. Nourish (BSA) 30m 13.6sec, 74.98mph

Even though Bernard was fastest overall in the Senior practice, and everyone was impressed with his performance so far, there was still room for small improvements. Geoff Duke had told him that the best way to go down Bray Hill was flat out and if he didn't, the bike wouldn't handle as well. Bernard was still reluctant to try this and would ease off the throttle a bit and, sure enough, because of the bumpy surface his weight was thrown forward and he got into a 'tank slapper', trapping his thumbs between the handlebars and the tank with petrol spilling everywhere. The first time he did it flat out the bike was a lot smoother and after that he said, *"it seemed so easy, and you thought nothing of it."*

David Merridan, the 28-year-old rider from High Wycombe, crashed at Ballaugh Bridge in this second practice session, when his BSA left the ground going over the bridge and landed awkwardly; the machine went violently out of control and Merridan hit a wall and was killed instantly.

In the Monday afternoon practice, Bernard went out on his 350cc BSA and again finished the session fastest in the Junior class.

Fastest 500cc Lap times (3rd Practice session)
1st D. Jervis (BSA) 27m 20sec, 82.85mph
2nd R.E. Jerrard (BSA) 27m 24.2sec, 82.65mph
3rd A.H. Jenkins (BSA) 28m 13.6sec, 80.23mph
4th P.K. Cruse (BSA) 28m 19.8sec, 79.91mph

5th M.T. Brookes (Triumph) 28m 31.6sec, 79.40mph
6th B.W. Newman (BSA) 28.59.0sec, 78.12mph

Fastest 350cc Lap times (3rd Practice session)
1ST B.D. Codd (BSA) 27m 56.4sec, 81.06mph
2nd J. Eckart (BSA) 28m 11sec, 80.35mph
3rd F. Wallis (BSA) 29m 06.4sec, 77.81mph
4th J.D Morton (BSA) 29m 28.6sec, 76.85mph
5th E. Unwin (BSA) 29m 31.8sec, 76.72mph
6th A. Shepherd (Norton) 29m 37sec, 76.46mph

After perfect weather conditions for the Practice sessions on Monday, Tuesday was completely different with a fresh north-easterly wind and at 4.45am, when the fourth session started, conditions were far from ideal. Low cloud was on the mountain, extending from the Gooseneck to Craig-ny-Baa, with visibility down to 20 yards but, despite these less-than-ideal conditions, lap times were still impressive. Bernard was on his 350cc BSA for the second time, and again posted the fastest time of the morning in the Junior class. R.E. Jerrard was the fastest in the Senior class.

Fastest 500cc Lap times (4th Practice session)
1st R.E. Jerrard (BSA) 27m 56.6sec, 81.04mph
2nd W.J. Hill (BSA) 28m 59.6sec, 78.04mph
3rd J.R. Hurlstone (Triumph) 29m 01.4sec, 78.00mph
4th M.T. Brookes (Triumph) 29m 03.6sec, 77.92mph
5th D. Hagen (BSA) 29m 37sec, 76.46mph
6th G. Coombes (BSA) 29m 50sec, 75.90mph

Fastest 350cc Lap times (4th Practice session)
1st B.D. Codd (BSA) 29m 17.2sec, 77.33mph
2nd A. Shepherd (Norton) 29m 52.2sec, 75.81mph
3rd D.H. Nourish (BSA) 30m 11.6sec, 74.99mph
4th D. Jervis (BSA) 30m 14.6sec, 74.88mph
5th N. Robertson (BSA) 30m 44.2sec, 73.68mph
6th D.D. Shand (BSA) 30m 48.6sec, 73.50mph

Bernard had proved with his impressive practice times on both the 350cc and 500cc machines that he was a serious contender for the wins, despite this being his first time racing the mountain circuit. His preparation for the races was second to none, and with the tuition he had received from three of the top names in motorcycle racing and the number of laps he had done before and throughout the run-up to race day he was ready, but no one was prepared for the impact he was about to make on the motorcycling world. Thursday 14th June 1956, the weather was perfect for racing, and there was continuous sunshine throughout the day.

The Clubman's TT was an event for roadgoing machines and therefore they had to be equipped accordingly, with accessories such as dynamos and headlamps, although the headlamps were covered for safety reasons. Air cleaners and luggage racks could be removed; side and centre stands could now be taken off the machines as well but were regarded compulsory when the Clubman's event was first run back in 1947. Everyone was pleased to see the Clubman's TT once again run on the mountain course after the 1955 event had been raced on the 10.79-mile Clypse circuit (which hadn't proved very popular with competitors), and this had showed with the drop in the number of entries for that year's event. This year there were 68 entries, 33 more than the previous year.

The Clubman races were run over three laps in 1956 instead of the four laps in 1954, which was the last time the race had been run on the 37.73-mile-long classic course. Past winners of this event included Geoff Duke, Alistair King, Denis Parkinson, and Derek Powell. You could say it was the first step for an up-and-coming rider on his quest to greater accolades in the motorcycling world in the 1940s and 50s.

Bernard was riding for the Louth & District Motorcycle Club, for the simple reason he explained years later in an interview:

> *"You had to be entered by a club, but because the Boston Club said it would take any money I won, I rode for the Louth Club instead. They said I could keep my winnings."*

He did however proudly wear the three crowns emblem on his crash helmet, which represented Boston Grammar School. He continued to do this throughout his racing career.

At 11.00am the first of the riders were on their away. One of the regulations of the Clubman event was that the machines had to be kick started so not everyone got a quick, clean start. Starting in groups of four at 30-second intervals, Bernard was in the second group and by the time he reached Ballacraine just over seven miles from the start he had caught P.G. Kirkham (BSA) who had been first away. At Kirkmichael he was in the lead. The commentator praised Bernard for his riding style as he passed Kepple Gate.

Bernard's first lap of 27m 30.4sec, which equated to an average speed of 82.33mph, was faster than any of his practice laps. P.G. Kirkham from Montgomeryshire crashed into a stone wall on his first lap at the Waterworks bend on the mountain climb and was killed instantly. He was thrown into the middle of the road and was discovered lying there by a marshal. News of his death was withheld until after the race so that his mother could be informed. At the end of the first lap the leader board showed:

1st B.D. Codd (BSA) 27m 30.4sec, 82.33mph
2nd J. Eckart (BSA) 28m 04.4sec, 80.65mph
3rd A. Shepherd (Norton) 28m 39.8sec, 79.05mph
4th D. Jervis (BSA) 28m 56.8sec, 78.22mph
5th E. Unwin (BSA) 29m 13.2sec, 77.49mph
6th J.D. Morton (BSA) 29m 15sec, 77.42mph

Bernard's second lap was almost three seconds slower than his first, but he still crossed the line with a commanding lead over John Eckart of 47sec. The leader board after lap two showed:

1st B.D. Codd (BSA) 55m 3.8sec, 82.23mph
2nd J. Eckart (BSA) 55m 51sec, 81.08mph
3rd A. Shepherd (Norton) 57m 5.4sec, 79.22mph
4th D. Jervis (BSA) 57m 34.8sec, 78.64mph
5th E. Unwin (BSA) 57m 41.8sec, 78.48mph
6th J.D. Morton (BSA) 57m 54.4sec, 78.20mph

Fast, smooth and with style, Bernard passed through Ramsey to start his climb over Snaefell, then through Creg-ny-Baa and Hillberry and on to Signpost Corner; round Governors Bridge onto the Glencrutchery Road and across the line for what turned out to be an easy win. He looked very calm, collected, and pleased with himself as he took his place in the winner's enclosure. In an interview after the race Bernard said *"I was riding under strict supervision, I enjoyed a relatively comfortable ride with only a momentary spot of bother on Bray Hill at the start of the second lap".* He went on to say *"I might have a chance of getting in the first three in the Senior. Ron Jerrard will win it."* The final order was:

1st B.D. Codd (BSA) 1h 22m 40.4sec, 82.02mph
2nd J. Eckart (BSA) 1h 23m 30sec, 81.34mph
3rd A. Shepherd (Norton) 1h 25m 43.2sec, 79.24mph

4th D. Jervis (BSA) 1h 26m 8sec, 78.86mph
5th E. Unwin (BSA) 1h 26m 8.8sec, 78.84mph
6th J.D. Morton (BSA) 1h 26m 21.2sec, 78.66mph

Out of the 68 entries, 55 started and 50 completed the race. All but two of the entries were BSA machines, the other two being A. Shepherd (Norton) who finished third and J.F. Righton (Velocette) who finished twenty-third.

The rules and regulations regarding the Clubman event demanded that the machines of the first three finishers were subjected to a post-race inspection. The engines were stripped down to confirm that no illegal modifications had been made, that all adjustments were correct and that all accessories that should function still did so. The brakes, chains and tyres showed very little sign of wear despite being raced hard for over 113-miles.

The fastest lap and Dunlop Trophy: B.D. Codd (BSA) on his first lap with a time of 27m 30.4sec a speed of 82.33mph.

Centre Team prize was won by East Midland Centre (B.D. Codd, F. Wallis and J. Eckart).

Bernard didn't have much time to enjoy his success after the Junior race win as he was back for the start of the Senior event in the afternoon which started at 2.00pm. The weather remained perfect for racing with just a slight breeze for the Senior race. Of the 43 entries only 32 were listed as starting. The race was started by Les Lumby, the timekeeper, when he dropped his flag, and the riders set off in groups of four at 30-second intervals, again kick-starting their machines.

By the time E. Minihan (499cc BSA), the last rider to leave the start line, had got away, Bernard was already at Ballacraine and leading. Ron Jerrard was also riding well and in second place on his 499cc BSA. As Bernard came past the grandstand to complete his first lap you could see by the look on Austin Munks face that it was a good lap time. It was recorded as 26m 15.2sec which was an average speed of 86.26mph and the first lap leader board was:

1st B.D. Codd (BSA) 26m 15.2sec, 86.26mph
2nd R. Jerrard (BSA) 26m 42.2sec, 84.81mph
3rd D. Jervis (BSA) 27m 16.4sec, 83.03mph

4th F. Wallis (BSA) 27m 28.6sec, 82.42mph
5th A.H. Jenkins (BSA) 27m 29sec, 82.40mph
6th M.T. Brookes (Triumph) 27m 53.2sec, 81.20mph

Bernard improved his lead on the second lap over Jerrard, with D. Jervis retiring from third place at Sulby Bridge with engine trouble, which promoted Fred Wallis into third place, and by the end of the lap Bernard had increased his lead to over one minute with a lap time of 26m 10.4sec, a speed of 86.52mph. The positions after lap two were:

1st B.D. Codd (BSA) 52m 25.6sec, 86.37mph
2nd R. Jerrard (BSA) 53m 13sec, 85.09mph
3rd F. Wallis (BSA) 54m 24.2sec, 83.29mph
4th A.H. Jenkins (BSA) 54m 22.4sec, 83.28mph
5th M.T. Brookes (Triumph) 55m 22.4sec, 81.78mph
6th D.J. Smart (BSA) 55m 44sec, 81.25mph

M.T. Brookes was catching Jenkins and Wallis on the final lap, but had a gearbox problem at The Bungalow, thereby losing his place on the leader board, and B. Payton (BSA) retired at the Gooseneck on the last lap. Bernard had no such trouble and was reported as riding *"swiftly and confidently"* by observers all around the course. He crossed the line for what turned out to be another comfortable win. A.H. Jenkins passed Fred Wallis in the last few miles of the race to finish third behind Ron Jerrard. M.T. Brookes pushed his Triumph across the line to finish twenty-sixth. The finishing order was:

1st B.D. Codd (BSA) 1h 18m 40.6sec, 86.33mph
2nd R.G. Jerrard (BSA) 1h 19m 46.8sec, 85.13mph
3rd A.H. Jenkins (BSA) 1h 21m 22.4sec, 83.47mph
4th F. Wallis (BSA) 1h 21m 24.2sec, 83.44mph
5th D.J. Smart (BSA) 1h 23m 15sec, 81.59mph
6th G. Coombes (BSA) 1h 24m 4.8sec, 80.78mph

Fastest lap and Dunlop trophy: B.D. Codd (BSA) (second lap) 26m 10.4sec, 86.52mph.

Centre Team Prize: Southern Centre (B.W. Newman, W.J. Hill, R.G. Jerrard) all riding BSA machines.
Again, the machines of the first three riders home were stripped down and

inspected, and again nothing untoward was found; in fact they were reported as looking in *"showroom condition"* with all controls, chains and tyres in good condition. Bernard's Gold Star was said to have been running slightly less rich than the other two.

After the race, Bernard was interviewed and was obviously delighted with his achievement of being the first man to win the "Double" on the same day in the history of the Clubman's event. Bernard went on to say *"I didn't win it – the machine won it for me. I had a trouble-free ride with literally no incidents."*

In the pits for Bernard was his father, Harold Codd, Sam Coupland and Austin Munks. His signalling station at Ginger Hall was manned by his youngest brother, Gerald Codd, Gordon Woodman of Holbeach and Jock Clark, a friend of Austin Munks. They would use the telephone at the pub to keep in contact with someone in a phone box at the grandstand. Bernard recalled in a later interview that he thought he won £200 in prize money for winning the two events. Bernard's mother, who had stayed at home to look after the family farm, told a Standard reporter *"I should have loved to see that laurel wreath go on the boy."*

At the prizegiving ceremony, held at The Villa Marina, the awards for both the Junior and Senior events were presented to Bernard by Sir Ralph Stevenson G.C.M.G, M.L.C.

Bernard also received the Dunlop trophies and Replicas for the fastest laps in both races, as well as being a member of the winning Centre Team with J. Eckart and Fred Wallis in the Junior event.

Sponsorship is a big part of modern-day sport, especially motorcycle racing, but back in the 1950s there was no evidence of this on the rider's leathers or on the machines. Bernard did, however, endorse Esso Petrol, Renold Chains and Castrol Oil.

In his speech, Bernard thanked everyone who had helped him and said that his ambition was to win the Senior International TT. Austin Munks was then asked to say a few words, and he spoke of rumours of *"non-standard"* parts being used on Bernard's machines. He went on to say that this was quite untrue, and anyone was welcome to examine the BSAs ridden by Bernard, and also to purchase any of the parts that had been used. Without a doubt, one advantage

Bernard did have over his competitors was having Sam Coupland preparing his bikes for him.

This was the last year the Clubman's TT was raced and the reasons for this decision are often disputed in motorcycling circles. One suggestion was that there was a lack of support for the event; others say that the rising costs of racing was a contributing factor, but the most often heard explanation was that with the obvious domination of the BSA Goldstar in this event their rival manufacturers such as Norton and AMC were tired of being humiliated by the success of the Goldstar year after year, and therefore put pressure on the ACU (Auto Cycle Union) to find a reason to stop the event taking place. No doubt - as in modern life - influential individuals with money can often sway a decision in their favour.

In winning the Junior and Senior races Bernard received free entries for the Manx Grand Prix, which was to be held in September.

Again, in an interview a few years later Bernard told how proud his father was of his achievements:

> *"I had never seen my father get drunk, only on that night. They had enough stuff for two receptions for two different winners. It all came to us! My father was drinking champagne, and they just kept coming round and filling him up. He got so drunk I had to take him home."*

Bernard was to receive another award a few days later, this time from "Sporting Record", a weekly sporting newspaper which selected him as one of two sporting personalities of the week. The other one was Lieut.Col F.W.C. Weldon, who captained the British Equestrian Team in the Olympic Games. Both received engraved cigarette lighters.

Peter Davey, who was the first private owner to finish in two International TT races and was a very experienced rider on circuits at home and abroad, said of Bernard: *"I think Codd is going to be a possible successor to Geoff Duke."* I don't think a rider at the beginning of his career could have received a better compliment than that.

The headline in the Louth Standard on 22nd June 1956 read:

"THEY CALL HIM THE BOSTON BOMBSHELL"

The report went on to say:

> *At 22 Bernard Codd of Wrangle has made sure of his name in the motorcycling record books by being the first rider ever to win two races on the same day over the famous Isle of Man Mountain course. This achievement of winning both Junior and Senior Clubman's TT races last Thursday earned him headlines in the National Press and made him a celebrity in the motorcycling world. He is already regarded as a successor to Geoff Duke and has been asked to be guest of honour at a dinner and open new showrooms in Liverpool. On his return home Bernard said, "I want to thank all the people who have helped me to success and to my two BSA's, they were marvellous." There was a long list of people not forgetting his father and mother, Mr and Mrs H. Codd who had never stood in the way of his motorcycling ambitions, indeed have given him every help and encouragement. Top of his thankyou list was Austin Munks the race wise general of innumerable motorcycle victories and Sam Coupland for preparing Bernard's Gold Stars for the Clubman's events.*
>
> *It was estimated that to date Sam Coupland had prepared machines for thirteen-star rides with thirteen finishes, nine firsts, two thirds, one fourth and a sixth. "If there was an award for the tuner of Isle of Man winning machines, and why isn't there? Then the quietly spoken, dryly humoured man from Frithville would be the first on the list. Sam is a man who won't go to bed until he is perfectly happy that all is well with the machine he is working on, then and only then will he consent to down tools and call it a day. His achievements are known and respected throughout the motorcycling world."*

Bernard was regarded as a local celebrity, and the fact that he was competing in the Isle of Man Clubman races was so important to the people of Wrangle that even the headmaster of the local school, Mr. Fred Barron, let the children listen to the races on the wireless in the classroom.

Bernard with his Matchless G9

Cadwell Park programme
2nd April, 1956

Snetterton programme
Sunday 8th April, 1956

Mallory Park programme
Sunday 13th May, 1956

Cadwell Park programme
Whit Monday 1956

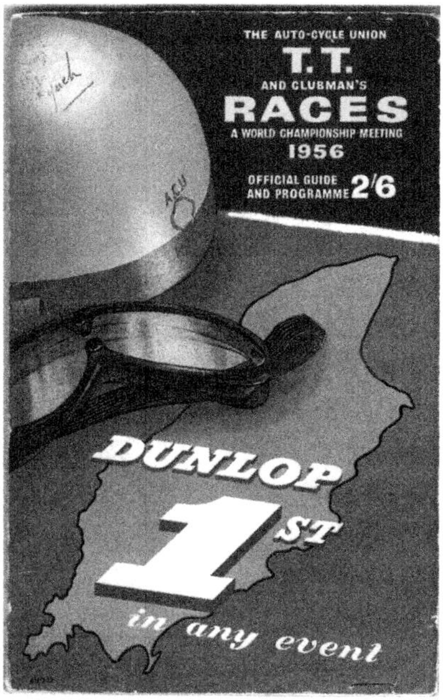

TT Races programme
1956

The start of the race and the epic battle between
Bernard (No 92) and George Catlin (No 1)
Cadwell Park 1956

Close racing between
Bernard and
George Catlin,
Cadwell Park 1956

Bernard head down
and full chat,
Cadwell Park
April 2nd, 1956

Bernard on the
500cc
Norton at
Cadwell Park 1956

Leading into the
hairpin on the 500cc
Norton at
Cadwell Park
1956

Exiting the
Hairpin on the
350cc Norton

More close
racing with
George Catlin
at
Cadwell Park
1956

Cadwell Park
Whit Monday 1956

Back in the paddock
Whit Monday 1956

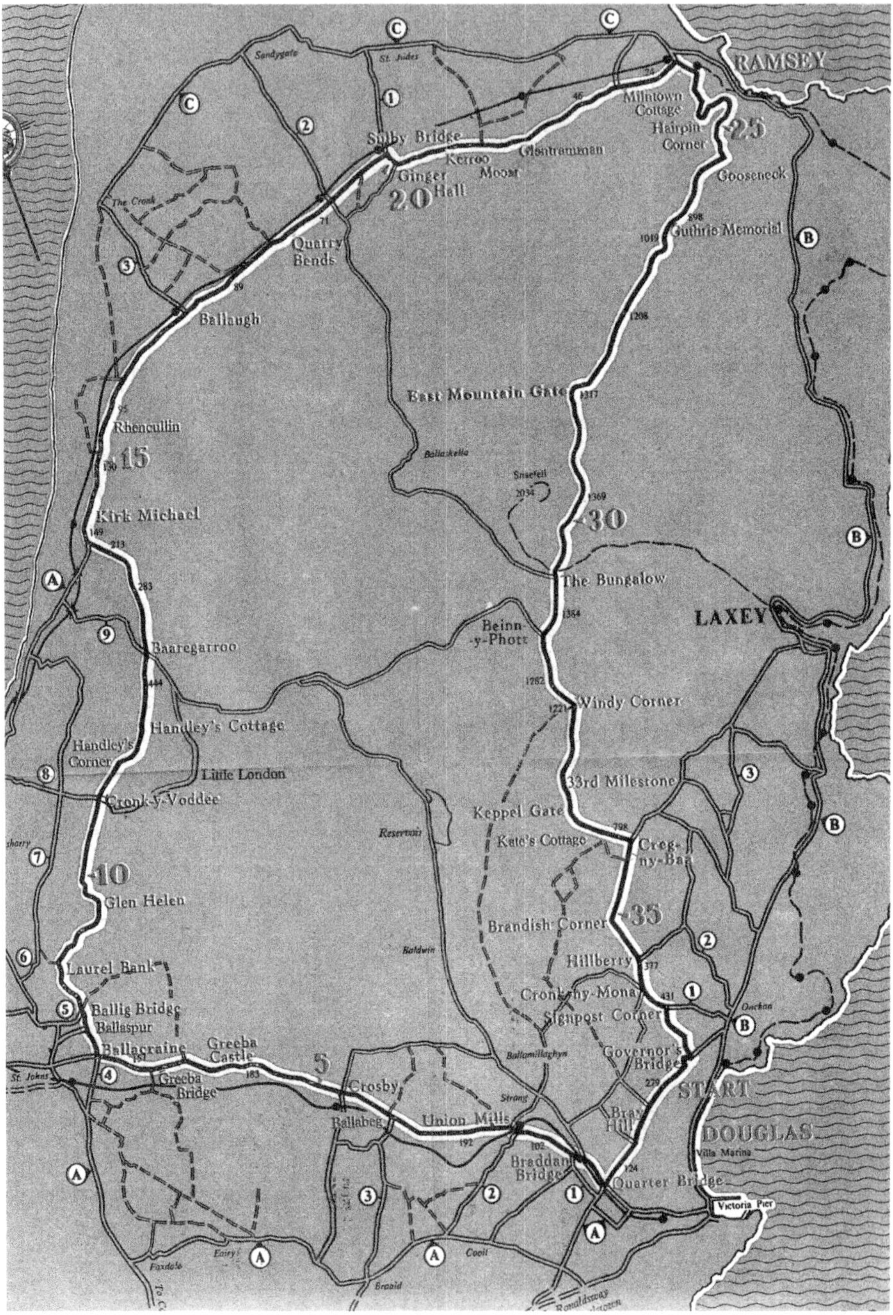

Map of the TT Circuit taken from the 1956 programme

On the 350cc BSA Gold Star in the Junior Clubmans TT

In the winner's enclosure after the Junior race with runner-up John Eckert (No 52) and third placed A. Shepherd (No 25)

Bernard
accelerating from
Laurel-Bank Bridge
on his way to
winning the
Senior Clubmans
TT on his
500cc
BSA Gold Star

Bernard
exiting the
Water-Works Corner
at the start of the
mountain section
in the Senior race

Bernard
on his way
to his
second win
of the day
in the
Clubmans TT

Bernard in the winner's enclosure after his record breaking second win in one day alongside second place Ron Jerrard (No 29) and third place Tony Jenkins (No 10)

Bernard,
Austin Munks
and Sam Coupland
with the
TT winning
BSA Gold Star

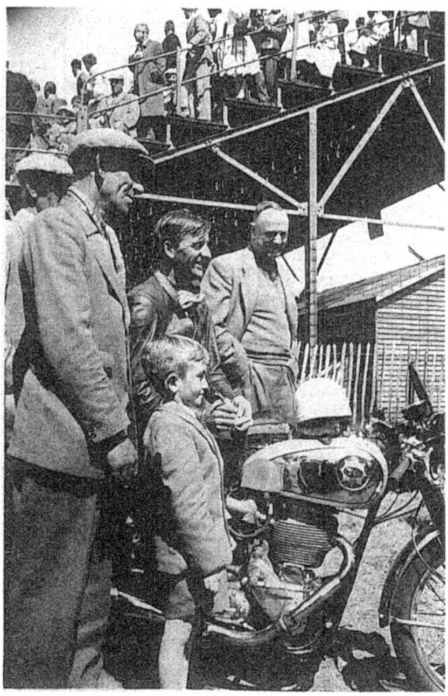

Bernard and
Sam Coupland

Portrait
photograph
of Bernard
after his
Clubmans
success

CHAPTER SIX

SHORT CIRCUITS AND THE MANX

"The perfect line"

Britain's longest race in 1956 was the Thruxton Nine-hour event, organised by the Southampton & District Motorcycle Club, and held on Saturday 23rd June. The aerodrome circuit at Thruxton, situated near Andover in Hampshire, was the ideal venue for such an event. The two-and-three-quarter-mile long circuit had challenging corners to test the skill of the riders, and long straights where the machines could achieve high speeds. As with the Clubman's event, these machines were standard models with a certain amount of tuning allowed and, again, the race was started with the riders kick-starting their machines.

Sixty riders competed in the race, which started at noon. In the 350cc class there were ten BSA Gold Stars, three Velocettes and a Matchless G3. In the 500cc class there were 22 BSAs, four Triumph T100s, a Norton model 88, a Velocette Venom and a Matchless G9. The 750cc class consisted of seven T110 Triumphs, two Royal Enfield Super-Meteors, a Norton Model 99 and a BSA A10.

Bernard was riding a BSA 499cc Gold Star and was teamed up with F.A. Rutherford. At the end of the first hour of racing the Codd-Rutherford partnership was leading with 28 laps completed. At the second hour mark, the lead had been taken by D.T. Powell and T. Godfrey riding a 350cc BSA Gold Star, having completed 53 laps. The riders were coming into the pits by this point for oil, petrol, tyres, and a change of rider. At the halfway stage the overall leading pair was K.W. James and I.I. Lloyd on a 350cc BSA Gold Star having completed 131 laps with an average speed of 72.24mph, including pit stops. They were closely followed by Powell and Godfrey. When the race finished at 9.00pm the overall winners were K.W. James and I.I. Lloyd on their 350cc BSA Gold Star. Bernard and F.W. Rutherford won the 500cc Class on their 499cc BSA Gold Star. The results were:

General classification and winners of "The Motorcycle Challenge Trophy"

1st K.W. James / I.I. Lloyd (350cc BSA)

2nd B.D. Codd / F.W. Rutherford 499cc BSA)

3rd H. Argent / E.P. Eacott (499ccBSA)
4th T. Godfrey / D.T. Powell (350cc BSA)
5th D.G. Chapman / W.J. Hill (499cc BSA)
6th R. Lawrence / G.H. Turner (499cc BSA)

350cc Class
1st K.W. James / I.I. Lloyd (BSA) 236 laps
2nd T. Godfrey / D.T. Powell (BSA) 230 laps
3rd R.A. Avery / F.G. Webber (BSA) 224 laps
4th J.W. Eckart / D.J. Smart (BSA) 224 laps
5th J.D. Hamilton / R.A. Wheeler (BSA) 216 laps
6th R.J. Langston / J.F. Righton (Velocette) 216 laps

500cc Class
1st B.D. Codd / F.A. Rutherford (BSA) 232 laps, average speed of 70.77mph
2nd H. Argent / E.P. Eacott (BSA) 231 laps, average speed of 70.47mph
3rd D.G. Chapman / W.J. Hill (BSA) 229 laps
4th R. Lawrence / G.H. Turner (BSA) 224 laps
5th R. Anderson / G. Stroud (BSA) 218 laps
6th B.L. Denehy / B.W. Newman (BSA) 217 laps

750cc Class
1st K. Bryen / P.H. Tait (Triumph) 222 laps
2nd J.W. Dakin / R. Erskin (BSA) 205 laps
3rd J.H.V. Allington / J.V. Hatcher (Triumph) 199 laps
4th G.J. Hughes / S.W. Stevens (Triumph) 197 laps
5th K.G. Buckmaster / J.A. Winfield (Triumph) 195 laps
6th J.E. Francis / D.H. Leckie (Triumph) 193 laps

The following day, 24th June, the Gravesend Eagles MCC organised an event at the Brands Hatch circuit in Kent. The races were run over the 1.24-mile-long track and was a competition between a team from Brands Hatch and a team from Cadwell Park. There was a crowd of over 10,000 to watch a good days racing.

Bernard didn't take part at this meeting but some of the riders that were at Thruxton the previous day did make the journey to compete. Bob McIntyre was entered as a member of the Cadwell Park team but was unable to ride due to recovering from an accident the previous day at Thruxton. I have included the results for this meeting as Bernard did participate in the second leg of this event, which was held at Cadwell Park the following week. The two teams were:

Brands Hatch Solo riders:
A. Trow (500cc Norton)
M.P. O'Rourke (499cc Norton)
F.Perris (348cc AJS)
E. Minihan (499cc Norton)
J.R. Clark (498cc Matchless)
D. Minter (499cc BSA)
J.L. Payne (499cc Norton)
G. Tanner (500cc Norton)
M.W. Saluz (499cc Norton)
E. Washer (349cc AJS)

Reserves:
F. Rutherford (498cc Norton)
R.S. Snell (498cc AJS)

Brands Hatch Sidecar Team:
O.E. Greenwood / T. Fairbrother (500cc Norton)
W. Boddice / W. Storr (499cc Norton)
A. Ellis / I. Paskin (499cc Norton)
E.T. Young / C.D. Young (498cc E.T.Y. Triumph)
Reserve:
P. Wollett / M.J. Candy (499cc Norton)

Cadwell Park Solo riders
R. McIntyre (500cc Norton)
A. King (499cc Norton)
F. Wallis (498cc Matchless)
A. Evans (499cc Norton)
J.B. Denton (499cc Norton)
G.A. Catlin (499cc Norton)
P.A. Davey (499cc BSA)
P. Ferbrache (499cc Norton)
J. Eckart (499cc Norton)
B. Freestone (499cc Norton)

Reserves:
J. Walker (650 S.C.S.)
R.H. Lilley (499cc Norton)

Cadwell Park Sidecar Team:
E. Walker / D.G. Roberts (499cc Norton)
J. Beeton / Unknown (499cc Norton)
F. Hanks / E. Dorman (498cc Matchless)
J.H.T. Harris / T. Plant (499cc Norton)
Reserve:
M.E. Wright / B. Rust (499cc Norton)

The invitation Team race was won by A. Trow (499cc Norton) with Derek Minter (499cc BSA) second. M.W. Saluz (499cc Norton) passed J. Clark (498cc Matchless) on lap six to finish third with M.P. O'Rourke (499cc Norton) also overtaking him to finish fourth. All the first four were representing the Brands Hatch Team. Fifth was the first Cadwell Park rider home, P. Ferbrache (499cc Norton). J. Clark (498cc Matchless) finished sixth, also representing the Brands Hatch team. J.R. Clark got his revenge in the final race of the day leading from start to finish in the 351cc -1000cc event. Following a bad start, Derek Minter fought his way up the leader board to finish second, just half a bike's length behind. M.P. O'Rourke, riding an MV Agusta in the 201cc -250cc event, got a terrible start but passed nine riders on the first lap and made his way up to eighth position on the second lap, third on the next lap, second on the fifth lap, was leading on the sixth lap and won by 30 yards. The results were:

201cc – 250cc Race (8 laps) 9.92 miles
1st M.P. O'Rourke (MV Agusta) 9m 15.6sec, 64.28mph
2nd R.S. Mayhew (Velocette)
3rd E. Minihan (NSU)
4th T. Thorp (BSA)

251cc – 350cc Race (10 laps) 12.4 miles
1st A. Trow (348cc Norton) 10m 50.4sec, 68.63mph
2nd J.R. Clark (348cc AJS)
3rd G.C.A. Murphy (348cc AJS)
4th E.J. Washer (349cc AJS)

Invitation Team Race (12 laps) 14.88 miles
1st A. Trow (499cc Norton- Brands Hatch) 12m 48.4sec, 69.71mph
2nd D. Minter (499cc BSA - Brands Hatch)
3rd M.W. Saluz (499cc Norton - Brands Hatch)
4th M.P. O'Rourke (499cc Norton - Brands Hatch)

1200cc Sidecar Race (8 laps)
1st W. Boddice (499cc Norton) 9m 21.8sec, 63.61mph
2nd E.T. Young (498cc E.T.Y. special)
3rd E. Walker (499cc Norton)
4th F. Hanks (498cc Matchless)

Sidecar Invitation Team Race (6 laps) 7.44 miles
1st W. Boddice (499cc Norton- Brands Hatch) 7m 1.2sec, 63.59mph
2nd E. Walker (499cc Norton - Cadwell Park)
3rd E.T. Young (498cc E.T.Y. special - Brands Hatch)
4th P. Wollett (499cc Norton - Brands Hatch)

351cc-1000cc Race (10 laps)
1st J.R. Clark (498cc Matchless) 10m 42.4sec, 69.49mph
2nd D. Minter (499cc BSA)
3rd M.P. O'Rourke (499cc Norton)
4th M.W. Saluz (499cc Norton

Team Contest scores after the first leg:
Brands Hatch 144 points Cadwell Park 98 points

On Saturday 30th June Boston Rural District Council (BRDC) paid tribute to Bernard for his *"Magnificent achievement"* in the Clubmans TT events in the Isle of Man. At their meeting on 30th June, Bernard was accompanied by Austin Munks and Sam Coupland. Proposed by Councillor G.H. Kime and seconded by Councillor W.M. Stanwell, the following resolution was passed:

> *"That B.R.D.C. records its recognition and highest appreciation of the magnificent achievement of Bernard Codd of Claxey Bank in the parish of Wrangle, on the 14th day of June 1956 when by his skill, prowess, and endurance against considerable opposition he won the Junior and Senior Clubmans Tourist Trophy motorcycle races over*

the Isle of Man course of 113.2 miles at record speeds of 82.02mph and 86.33mph respectively. Thereby bringing distinction, international fame, and honour not only directly upon himself but indirectly upon the Rural District of Boston, in the area of which he is an honoured resident"

A copy of the resolution bearing the common seal of the Council was presented to Bernard. Proposing the resolution, Councillor Kime said it was with the greatest possible pleasure that he offered Mr. Codd, on behalf of the Council, hearty congratulations. He also mentioned Austin Munks and Sam Coupland, whose support and encouragement had done much in contributing towards Bernard's success, commenting that it was an honour to be in the presence of three men distinguished in motor cycling realms. Presenting the copy of the resolution The Chairman, Councillor A. Fyson, said:

> *"Mr. Codd has won cups, but lots of people had cups, but it was not everyone had what they were presenting him, this was an honour not conferred lightly - not even to Chairmen of the Council."* Bernard replied by saying *"I would like to thank you for your presentation. I am proud to have won these races on behalf of Boston and the Rural District."*

I would like to know what Bernard really thought to this, and I would also like to know if The Boston Club now regretted the fact that Bernard felt the need to race for the Louth Club and not theirs.

The second leg of the Brands Hatch v Cadwell Park contest was held at Cadwell Park on Sunday July 1st. Both teams were slightly different to the first leg, and the Brands Hatch Team listed in the programme was:

Brands Hatch Solo riders:
D. Minter (499cc BSA)
G.B. Tanner (499cc Norton)
E.J. Washer (499cc Norton)
J.L. Payne (499cc Norton)
R.S. Snell (498cc AJS)
M.W. Saluz (499cc Norton)
F.G. Perris (348cc AJS)
E. Minihen (499cc Norton)

M.P. O'Rourke (499cc Norton)
A.J. Trow (499cc Norton)

Reserves:
F.A. Rutherford (499cc BSA)
G.A. Murphy (499cc Matchless)

Brands Hatch Sidecar Team:
O.E. Greenwood / T. Fairbrother (499cc Norton)
A. Ellis / I. Paskin (499cc Norton)
E.T. Young / C.D. Young (498cc Triumph)
W.G. Boddice / W. Storr (498cc Norton)
Reserve:
F. Taylor / R. Taylor (499cc Norton)

Cadwell Park Solo riders:
G.A. Catlin (499cc Norton)
P.A. Davey (499cc BSA)
F. Wallis (498cc Matchless)
A. Evans (499cc Norton)
P. Ferbrache (499cc Norton)
B.D. Codd (499cc Norton)
B. Freestone (499cc Norton)
J. Eckart (499cc Norton)
A. King (499cc Norton)
H. Plews (499cc Norton)
Reserves:
J.P. Hodkin (348cc BSA)
J. Walker (499cc S.C.S.)
R.H. Lilley (499cc Norton)

Cadwell Park Sidecar Team:
J. Beeton / C. Billingham or L. Nutt (499cc Norton)
F. Hanks / E. Dorman (498cc Matchless)
E. Walker / D. Roberts (499cc W.R. Norton)
J.H.T. Harris / T. Plant (499cc Norton)
Reserve:
R.E. Cheney / J. Fox (490cc Norton JAP)

The Sidecar Team Challenge race saw Bill Boddice get a good start on his Norton outfit, leading from Fred Hanks (Matchless) and Jack Beeton (Norton). Beeton passed Hanks on lap five, and E. Walker finished fourth. J.T. Harris (Norton) and E.T. Young riding an ultra-low Triumph twin outfit battled for fifth place, frequently swapping positions with the advantage eventually going Young's way. Cadwell scored 21 points and Brands Hatch scored 14 points. The result was:

Cadwell Park v Brands Hatch Sidecar Scratch Race Final (8 laps)
1st W.G. Boddice (498cc Norton – Brands Hatch) 11m 26sec, £20.00
2nd J. Beeton (499cc Norton – Cadwell Park) £15.00
3rd F. Hanks (498cc Matchless – Cadwell Park) £10.00
4th E. Walker (499cc W.R. Norton – Cadwell Park) £6.00

In the first heat of the Solo Team Challenge, George Catlin, P. Ferbrache and P.A. Davey finished in that order scoring top points for the Cadwell Team. In the second heat, Bernard won with B. Freestone second and A.J. Trow scoring third place points for the Brands Hatch Team. Points were awarded for both heats and Cadwell were coming out on top 17-4 in heat one and 15-6 in heat two.

The 12-lap final was led by J. Eckart (499cc Norton) who had only managed to finish sixth in his heat. He led for the first three laps at the end of which the order was Eckart, Catlin, Ferbrache and Bernard, (all Cadwell riders). Catlin passed Eckart on lap four as did Ferbrache, demonstrating the superior power of the Manx Norton. Bernard was also closing in and eventually passed Eckart to move up into third place. On lap nine Bernard had caught and passed Ferbrache, and on the approach to the mountain bends he briefly pulled out and passed Catlin but was offline for the second bend and Catlin retook the lead and went on to win in a wheel-to-wheel battle to the chequered flag. The result was:

Cadwell Park v Brands Hatch Solo Final (12 laps)
1st G. Catlin (499cc Norton – Cadwell Park) 14m 40.4sec, £15.00
2nd B.D. Codd (499cc Norton - Cadwell Park) £12.00
3rd P. Ferbrache (499cc Norton - Cadwell Park) £10.00
4th A.J. Trow (499cc Norton - Brands Hatch) £8.00

The result of the Cadwell Park v Brands Hatch Team Challenge on the day was Cadwell Park 107 points and Brands Hatch 47 points so Cadwell won the overall competition on aggregate 205 points to 191 points.

There was also a full programme of other races held that day and in the first heat of the Junior event Bernard won in a time of 7m 54.8sec on his 348cc Norton. In the final, P. Ferbrache (PF JAP) got away from the start line first but was soon caught and passed by Bernard, and by the end of lap two B. Freestone had also passed Ferbrache who was now being chased by Alistair King (349cc Norton). Freestone passed Bernard on lap four and King passed Ferbrache. Freestone led for the next three laps. On lap seven Bernard hit the front and he and Freestone pulled away from King and Trow in third and fourth places. George Catlin had a terrible start, but he did manage to pass Ferbrache and finish fifth.

350cc Solo Final (8 laps)
1st B.D. Codd (348cc Norton) 10m 10sec, £15.00
2nd B. Freestone (348cc Norton) £10.00
3rd A. King (349cc Norton) £8.00
4th A.J. Trow (348cc Norton) £6.00
5th G. Catlin (348cc Norton)

In the Senior Solo Final, the first five riders away were G. Catlin (499cc Norton) E.R. Fitton (499cc Norton) J.P. Hodgkin (348cc BSA) J. Eckart (499cc Norton) and Bernard (499cc Norton). They howled round Coppice Corner pulling away from the rest of the field. By lap three the pace had settled down and G. Catlin was leading Bernard by the smallest of margins, and Freestone was third. Entering Coppice Hill on lap five Catlin was leading but, on the swoop down to the Mountain, Bernard had taken the lead and had even opened a gap. Freestone caught and passed Catlin going up Coppice Hill on the next lap while King and Davey passed Hodgkin. Eckart and Ferbrache completed the field.

Senior Solo Final (8 laps)
1st B.D. Codd (499cc Norton) 10m 3.2sec, £15.00
2nd B. Freestone (499cc Norton) £10.00
3rd G.A. Catlin (499cc Norton) £8.00
4th P.A. Davey (499cc BSA) £4.00

250cc Solo Final (8 laps)
1st P.H. Tait (248cc Velocette) 11m 43.6sec
2nd G. Monty (248cc G.M.S.)
3rd R. Jones (249cc Triumph)
4th A.G. Briggs (249cc Triumph)

Sidecar Scratch Final (8 laps)

1st F. Taylor / R. Taylor (499cc Norton) 11m 6.4sec, £15.00
2nd J.W. Beevers / Unknown (499cc Norton-Watsonian) £10.00
3rd R.A. Robinson / L.P. Young (499cc Norton) £8.00
4th F.C. Pusey / J. Morris (499cc BSA) £4.00

Sidecar Handicap Final (8 laps)

1st A. Ellis / I. Paskin (499cc Norton) 11m 51.8sec, £15.00
2nd C. Freeman / T. Leak (499cc Norton) £10.00
3rd F. Hanks / E. Dorman (498cc Matchless) £8.00
4th J.W.T. Harris / T. Plant (499cc Norton) £4.00

Oliver's Mount circuit in Scarborough was Bernard's next meeting. The 2.43-mile road racetrack was - and still is - the only racetrack on mainland Britain to run on public roads. This two-day meeting, held on Friday 6th and Saturday 7th July, was organised by The Scarborough & District Motor Club Ltd with support from The Yorkshire Evening Post and The Yorkshire Post. This was the first chance to show off the recently built control tower on the start and finish straight, which was home to the officials and motorcycling press. The building had already been called "The house that Jack built" in recognition of Jack Claxton, clerk of the course, Club secretary and designer of the building.

Friday evening's race programme consisted of the eliminating heats and final of the 350cc class and two sidecar heats. In heat one of the 350cc class J. Eckart (BSA) took an early lead from G. Catlin (Norton) who lost a lot of ground on the opening lap, with P.H. Carter (Norton) third. A couple of laps later Catlin passed Eckart to take the lead, but he was soon passed by Carter who went on to win. Catlin finished second, R. Jervis (Norton) was third while J. Eckart, who was suffering with clutch trouble, finished a disappointed sixth.

Heat two was won by D.V. Chadwick (Norton), second was R. Anderson with A. King (Norton) third. Bernard was entered in heat three with J. Buchan (Norton), E. Mc Haldane (BSA), B. Freestone (Norton) and S.T. Barnett (Norton). B. Freestone took the lead from the start and was pushed hard by Bernard and Sid Barnett. J. Buchan passed Barnett on lap three and Bernard on lap four to secure second place behind Freestone. Bernard lost another place to G.E. Washer (AJS) when he missed a gear and Washer took advantage.

In the final, G. Catlin got away first followed by B. Freestone, and these two battled for 12 laps of the 15-lap race before D.V. Chadwick passed them both to go on and win comfortably.

Saturday was a typical race day at Oliver's Mount. The morning started off misty and dismal with visibility down to 50 yards, so riders had to be especially cautious on what was a challenging circuit even in dry, clear conditions. The first race was the 250cc event, won by P.H. Tait (248cc Velocette) with T.E. Fenwick (248cc Moto Guzzi) second.

In the 350cc scratch event the 16 second-fastest finishers from the 350cc heats were entered in this ten-lap race. H. Plews (Norton) led but was constantly challenged by D.A. Tutty (Norton). F. Wallis (BSA) was holding third place. It looked as though it was going to be an easy win for Plews, but G.B. Tanner (Norton) came through the field to take second place and start to put pressure on the leader. On the penultimate lap Tanner took the lead and the victory, also achieving the fastest lap.

There were three 500cc heats, the first won by Phil Carter (Norton) with B. Purslow (Norton) second and P.A. Davey (BSA) third. The second heat saw Bernard determined to make up for his bad luck in the 350cc event, but it was Fred Wallis (BSA) who set a fast early pace chased by A. King (Norton). Bernard was in third place battling with B. Freestone (Norton). Eventually Bernard caught King and the two of them had a closely fought contest for two laps with just a few feet separating them. At Memorial bend on the final lap Bernard tried to pass Alistair King but made an error and crashed out of the race. Fred Wallis finished second behind King. Bernard returned to the paddock area after the race with a broken left handlebar, but he had the consolation that he achieved the fastest lap of the race on lap five with a time of 2m 19sec.

In heat three R. Anderson (Norton) passed the early leader G. Catlin (Norton) on lap four and pulled away, winning by 35sec and achieving the fastest heat and lap time of the 500cc event. The results were:

250cc Scratch race final "The Jaconelli Trophy" (10 laps)
1st P.H. Tait (249cc Velocette) 27m 26.2sec, 52.78mph
2nd T.E. Fenwick (248cc Moto Guzzi)
3rd A.A. Williams (248cc Moto Guzzi)
Fastest lap: P.H. Tait (249cc Velocette) & T.E. Fenwick (248cc Moto Guzzi) 2m 41sec, 53.7mph

350cc Scratch race "Boothby Trophy" (10 laps)
1st G.B. Tanner (348cc Norton) 26m 0.4sec, 55.68mph
2nd H. Plews (348cc Norton)
3rd R. Fay (348cc BSA)
Fastest lap: G.B. Tanner (348cc Norton) 2m 27sec, 59.11mph

350cc Final "Whitaker Trophy" (15 laps)
1st D.V. Chadwick (348cc Norton) 34m 44.8sec, 62.64mph
2nd P.H. Carter (348cc Norton)
3rd B. Freestone (348cc Norton)
Fastest lap: D.V. Chadwick (348cc Norton) 2m 15.8sec, 63.98mph

350cc or 500cc Scratch Race "Grande Trophy" (10 laps)
1st T.S. Shepherd (499cc Norton) 23m 31sec, 61.58mph
2nd J. Eckart (499cc Norton)
3rd R. Cousins (499cc Norton)
Fastest lap: T.S. Shepherd (499cc Norton) 2m 17.4sec, 63.24mph

500cc Final "Tessyman Trophy" (15 laps)
1st P.H. Carter (499cc Norton) 33m 55.8sec, 64.02mph
2nd G.B. Tanner (499cc Norton)
3rd F.A. Rutherford (499cc BSA)
Fastest lap: R. Anderson (499cc Norton) 2m 12.2sec, 65.75mph

500cc Sidecar Final "The Scarborough Chamber of Trade Trophy" (7 laps)
1st F. Taylor (499cc Norton) 18m 17.8sec, 55.40mph
2nd F. Hanks (498cc Matchless)
3rd P. Woolett (499cc Norton)
Fastest lap: F. Taylor (499cc Norton) 2m 31sec, 57.32mph

Club Team Prize: Louth & D.M.C.
B.D. Codd, G.A. Catlin, B. Freestone (Best average 61.32mph in 350cc Class)

On July 14th at the Annual Wrangle Show, Bernard's two winning BSA machines from the Clubmans TT were on display, but the report doesn't mention whether Bernard attended the show or not.

Although there were meetings at Castle Combe on July 14th, Oulton Park on August 4th and Snetterton on August 5th, I can't find any mention of Bernard racing at any of these events. The next time he does appear is at Cadwell Park on August 6th (Bank Holiday Monday).

This was a mixed motorcycle and car meeting watched by an estimated 16,000 spectators. The weather was perfect for racing and Bernard made the most of it, breaking the six-and eight-lap records for the circuit in the 350cc event. Bernard won heat one of the 350cc class, improving John Surtees's previous lap record for the six-lap race (which Surtees recorded in the September 1955 meeting) by 2.8sec. Bernard's time was 7m 33.4sec in the eight-lap final. Bernard was lapping at an unbelievable pace of around 73sec which gave him a total race winning time of 9m 51.8sec.

In the sidecar scratch event John Harris (499cc Norton) won heat one, but Alf Ellis (499cc Norton) was not so fortunate, overturning his outfit in the woodland section, and was taken to hospital with a suspected fractured leg. E.T. Young (498cc Triumph) worked hard to battle his way to the front to win heat two. In the final J. Harris (Pip Harris's brother) was victorious with C. Freeman (499cc Norton) second and R. E. Cheney (497cc Norton) third.

Bernard won his heat in the Coronation Cup event as did G. Catlin (499cc Norton) and B. Freestone (499cc Norton). In the 12-lap final G. Catlin led Bernard for the first six laps when Bernard overshot the corner at the bottom of the Mountain losing three places which he failed to get back. G. Catlin increased his lead now over A. King (499cc Norton) and B. Freestone (499cc Norton). As a result of winning this race Catlin achieved the best 8-lap time of the year, qualifying for the Folbigg Trophy which was to be run on Sunday 16th September. He also joined a trio of unlimited cc lap record holders with a lap time of 1m 11sec, which he posted on his third and fifth laps. The other three - Rudy Allison, Peter Davey and Brian Freestone - established their times at the Easter 1956 meeting. The results were:

250cc Final (8 laps)
1st J. Eckart (249cc Excelsior) 10m 46.2sec, 55.6mph £10.00
2nd J. Murgatroyd (249cc Beasley Velocette) £6.00
3rd A.T. Barnwell (249cc Rudge) £3.00
4th J. Sims (249cc Velocette) £2.00
Fastest lap: J. Eckart (249cc Excelsior) 1m 18.4sec, 57.4mph

350cc Final (8 laps)
1st B.D. Codd (348cc Norton) 9m 51.8sec, 60.8mph £20.00
2nd B. Freestone (348cc Norton) £12.00
3rd K.H. Patrick (348cc BSA) £7.00
Fastest lap and new lap record: B.D. Codd (348cc Norton) 1m 11.6sec, 63mph

1000cc Coronation Cup Final (12 laps)
1st G. Catlin (499cc Norton) 14m 38.6sec, 61.7mph £25.00
2nd A. King (499cc Norton) £15.00
3rd B. Freestone (499cc Norton) £10.00
Fastest lap: G. Catlin (499cc Norton) 1m 11sec, 63.4mph

Sidecar Scratch Race Final (8 laps)
1st J.H.T. Harris / T. Plant (499cc Norton) 10m 52.6sec, 55.2mph £25.00
2nd E.T. Young / C.D. Young (498cc Triumph) £15.00
3rd C. Freeman / T. Leek (499cc Norton) £10.00
4th R.E. Cheney / J. Fox (497cc Norton) £6.00
Fastest lap: J.H.T. Harris / T. Plant (499cc Norton) 20sec, 56.25mph

Sidecar Handicap Race Final (8 laps)
1st C.H.R. Warner / C. Bullock (498cc Vincent) 11m 53.6sec, 51mph £15.00
2nd J.H.T. Harris / T. Plant (499cc Norton) £10.00
3rd E.T. Young / C.D. Young (498cc Triumph) £8.00
Fastest lap: J.H.T. Harris / T. Plant (499cc Norton) 1m 19.8sec, 56.3mph

The first practice day for The Manx Grand Prix of 1956 was on Wednesday 29th August and started at 6am. Due to rain the previous day the roads were still wet, especially under the trees, and it was reported by the Marshals that there was mist on the Mountain, which slowly thickened resulting in the session being stopped for 30 minutes. Bernard, out on his 499cc Norton, was reported as being *"Most impressive, safe, fast and very sure of his line"* by the Marshal at Quarter Bridge. Alistair King posted the fastest Senior lap of the first session with a speed of 88.53mph. This was achieved on his practice bike; his race bike was reported as being much faster. The practice times at the end of the first day were:

Senior Practice times (Wednesday 29th)
1st A King (Norton) 25m 35sec, 88.53mph
2nd E.M. Haldane (Norton) 26m 27sec, 85.63mph

3rd J. Drysdale (Norton) 26m 42sec, 84.82mph
4th E.J. Washer (Norton) 26m 46sec, 84.60mph
5th A. Shepherd (Norton) 26m 48sec, 84.50mph
6th W.A. Holmes (Norton) 26m 50sec, 84.39mph

Junior Practice times (Wednesday 29th)
1st R.H.F. Anderson (Norton) 26m 46sec, 84.60mph
2nd E.B. Crooks (Norton) 27m 09sec, 83.40mph
3rd R. Dowty (Norton) 27m 24sec, 82.65mph
4th T.R. Graham (Norton) 27m 39sec, 81.91mph
5th B.D. Codd (Norton) 27m 48sec, 81.46mph
6th K.H. Patrick (BSA) 27m 53sec, 81.21mph

The riding styles of the riders were observed at certain positions round the course, one of these sections being Hillberry. The riders that stood out from the others were A. King (Norton) who, it was said, was *"extremely fast"* and Bernard who had *"The perfect line."* It was said that some officials considered Bernard was trying to fox his opponents, as they were convinced he could go much faster. There were 111 riders out for the next session completing 185 laps between them, the fastest of these made by J. Buchan (Norton) with a speed of 90.50mph. Bernard was joint second fastest with Alastair King in the Senior and third fastest in the Junior.

Senior Practice times (Thursday 30th)
1st J. Buchan (Norton) 25m 01sec, 90.50mph
2nd = A. King (Norton) / B.D. Codd (Norton) 25m 07mph, 90.15mph
4th A. Shepherd (Norton) 25m 25sec, 89.11mph
5th E.F.H. Boyce (Norton) 25m 30sec, 88.82mph
6th W.A. Holmes (Norton) 25m 44sec, 88.01mph

Junior Practice times (Thursday 30th)
1st W.A. Holmes (Norton) 25m 25sec, 89.11mph
2nd A. King (Norton) 25m 48sec, 87.77mph
3rd B.D. Codd (Norton) 26m 36sec, 85.14mph
4th E.B. Crooks (Norton) 26m 39sec, 84.98mph
5th E.J. Washer (AJS) 26m 43sec, 84.77mph
6th T.R. Graham (Norton) 26m 44sec, 84.71mph

Friday morning's exciting practice session was overshadowed by the fatal accident of Maurice W. Saluz. He crashed at Sulby Bridge where it is thought that he was dazzled by the sun as he approached the bridge at speed down Sulby Straight. He tried to run off through an open gate - which was left open for such an eventuality - but misjudged it and hit the gate post. This was his first time on the Isle of Man, and he had only completed nine laps of the course.

Senior Practice times (Friday 31st)
1st A. King (Norton) 24m 41sec, 91.75mph
2nd E.J. Washer (Norton) 25m 20sec, 89.40mph
3rd E.B. Crooks (Norton) 25m 41sec, 88.18mph
4th = W.A. Holmes (Norton) / E.M. Haldane (Norton) 25m 49sec, 87.72mph
6th K.H. Patrick (BSA) 26m 22sec, 85.89mph

Junior Practice times (Friday 31st)
1st J. Buchan (Norton) 26m 36sec, 85.14mph
2nd B.D. Codd (Norton) 84.71mph
3rd T.R. Graham (Norton) 27m 33sec, 82.05mph
4th F.A. Rutherford (BSA) 27m 36sec, 82.02mph
5th B.L. Turner (Norton) 27m 38sec, 81.96mph
6th A.H. Jenkins (Norton) 27m 45sec, 81.61mph

Saturday's practice started at 6.10am and conditions were perfect, which showed in some excellent lap times. The fastest was R.H.F. Anderson (Norton); he lapped at a time of 24m 19sec, 93.14mph, equalling the Manx Grand Prix record that had been set the previous year by Geoff Tanner. Again, Bernard's style and speed on the 499cc Norton was noticed around the course, especially at Craig-Ny- Baa.

Senior Practice times (Saturday 1st)
1st R.H.F. Anderson (Norton) 24m 19sec, 93.14mph
2nd E.M. Haldane (Norton) 25m 14sec, 89.75mph
3rd A. Shepherd (Norton) 25m 25sec, 89.11mph
4th E.B. Crooks (Norton) 25m 37sec, 88.41mph
5th B.D. Codd (Norton) 25m 57sec, 87.25mph
6th E.J. Washer (Norton) 26m 01sec, 87.02mph

Junior Practice times (Saturday 1st)
1st A. King (Norton) 25m 37sec, 88.41mph
2nd B.D. Codd (Norton) 26m 43sec, 84.77mph
3rd E.F.H. Boyce (Norton) 26m 56sec, 84.07mph
4th T.R. Graham (Norton) 27m 06sec, 83.33mph

5th W.A. Holmes (Norton) 27m 11sec, 83.30mph
6th A.H. Jenkins (Norton) 27m 15sec, 83.10mph

The final practice on Monday 3rd September was spoilt by the weather: the track was wet all round the course and visibility was down to 50 yards. The last practice session was never a time to register fast laps, more a chance to make sure tyres and chains were run in and the machine was as race ready as possible. Despite the bad weather and poor track conditions there was only one incident reported when J.R. Hurlstone (348cc Norton) crashed when his bike skidded at Ballacraine. He escaped injury and was able to ride his Norton back to the paddock area. The fastest Senior lap was posted by R. Dowty (Norton) who achieved an average speed of 81.96mph. Bernard was in the top six in both classes and was considered as an outside favourite along with J. Buchan (Norton), R. Dowty (Norton), A. King (Norton), and F.A. Rutherford who was riding the BSA owned by Geoff Duke.

Senior Practice times (Monday 3rd)
1st R. Dowty (Norton) 27m 38sec, 81.96mph
2nd J. Drysdale (Norton) 28m 06sec, 80.58mph
3rd A. Shepherd (Norton) 28m 37sec, 79.14mph
4th A. King (Norton) 28m 55sec, 78.30mph
5th E.F.H. Boyce (Norton) 28m 58sec, 78.16mph
6th B.D. Codd (Norton) 29m 44sec, 76.16mph

Junior Practice times (Monday 3rd)
1st J. Buchan (Norton) 29m 19sec, 77.24mph
2nd R. Dowty (Norton) 29m 24sec, 77.03mph
3rd R.H.F. Anderson (Norton) 30m 15sec, 74.86mph
4th E.F.H. Boyce (Norton) 30m 25sec, 74.45mph
5th B.D. Codd (Norton) 30m 31sec, 74.21mph
6th B.J. Thompson (AJS) 30m 35sec, 74.05mph

Junior MGP (Tuesday 4th September)

The conditions were perfect for racing on race day. It was warm and sunny with a light breeze and visibility on the Mountain was reported as good. The race was started at 10.45am by Geoff Tanner, who was the previous year's winner of the Junior event. First rider away was R. Castle (AJS). R.H.F. Anderson set a good pace on the first lap and at the Ramsey timing point he was ahead of A. King but by the end of lap one King had made up nearly 30 sec on Anderson and was leading the race by 9.8sec. His time was 25m 7sec which was 11sec quicker than the existing lap record. W.A. Holmes was third, J. Buchan fourth and Bernard fifth. The leader board after lap one was:

1st A. King (Norton) 25m 07sec, 90.15mph
2nd R.H.F. Anderson (Norton) 25m 16.8sec, 89.58mph
3rd W.A. Holmes (Norton) 25m 34.8sec, 88.54mph
4th J. Buchan (Norton) 25m 56sec, 87.31mph
5th B.D. Codd (Norton) 26m 0.6sec, 86.75mph
6th E.B. Crooks (Norton) 26m 15.6sec, 86.25mph

Alastair King increased his lead over Anderson on the second lap and shattered his previous lap record with a speed of 91.07mph. Anderson made a pit stop at the end of the second lap for petrol, losing 30sec. W.A. Holmes was still third and J. Buchan fourth. Bernard also stopped at the pits at the end of lap two for petrol, losing 29sec. The lap two leader board was:

1st A. King (Norton) 49m 58.8sec, 90.60mph
2nd R.H.F. Anderson (Norton) 50m 32.8sec, 89.59mph
3rd W.A. Holmes (Norton) 51m 02sec, 88.13mph
4th J. Buchan (Norton) 51m 25.4sec, 88.06mph
5th B.D. Codd (Norton) 52m 07.6, 86.87mph
6th E.B. Crooks (Norton) 52m 09.4sec, 86.82mph

Anderson's pit stop meant that he lost second place to W.A. Holmes and Bernard dropped back to seventh after his stop. After lap three the positions were:

1st A. King (Norton) 1h 15m 09.6sec, 90.37mph
2nd W.A. Holmes (Norton) 1h 16m 25sec, 88.88mph
3rd R.H.F. Anderson (Norton) 1h 16m 45.4sec, 88.49mph
4th J. Buchan (Norton) 1h 16m 51.2sec, 88.37mph
5th E.B. Crooks (Norton) 1h 18m 07.2sec, 86.94mph
6th R. Dowty (Norton) 1h 18m 42.4sec, 86.30mph

Alastair King was consistently lapping at over 90mph and lost only 18sec with his pit stop for fuel. The fastest fuel stop of the race was K.H. Patrick (BSA) who was in twelfth place; he was stationary for just 12sec. The positions after lap four were:

1st A. King (Norton) 1h 40m 57.8sec, 89.70mph
2nd R.H.F. Anderson (Norton) 1h 42m 14.8sec, 88.57mph
3rd J. Buchan (Norton) 1h 42m 43.8sec, 88.16mph
4th E.B. Crooks (Norton) 1h 44m 29.6sec, 86.68mph
5th B.D. Codd (Norton) 1h 45m 07.8sec, 86.14mph
6th R. Dowty (Norton) 1h 45m 22.6sec, 85.94mph

Alastair King and Robert Anderson both retired on lap five, which put Jimmy Buchan on top of the leader board with an advantage of 2m 10sec over second place man E.B. Crooks. R. Dowty was third. Bernard had moved back up to fourth ahead of F.A. Rutherford on his BSA. Bernard was the first of the leading riders to begin the last lap, but no one took any unnecessary risks on this lap as they all had a reasonable gap between each other to be able to cruise home in those positions. Bernard crossed the line at 1.23pm to finish in a very creditable fourth place, which was an amazing result for Bernard because after the race it was discovered that the screw holding the jet needle had dropped into the jet, causing the engine to lose a certain amount of power. The first three home were J. Buchan, E.B. Crooks, and R. Dowty, all riding Nortons. The result was:

1st J. Buchan (Norton) 2h 33m 25sec, 88.54mph
2nd E.B. Crooks (Norton) 2h 35m 59sec, 87.09mph
3rd R. Dowty (Norton) 2h 37m 14.6sec, 86.39mph
4th B.D. Codd (Norton) 2h 37m 37.6sec, 86.18mph
5th F.A Rutherford (BSA) 2h 38m 08.6sec, 85.89mph
6th E.F.H. Boyce (Norton) 2h 38m 53.6sec, 85.49mph

Fastest lap: A. King (Norton) second lap 24m 51.8sec, 91.07mph
(New lap record)
Replicas were awarded to the first 28 riders to finish
(under 2h 48m 46sec)

The Club Team prize
The Winsford Club,
E.F.H. Boyce (Norton) G.D. Allcock (BSA)
J.R. Hurlstone (Norton)

Senior MGP (Thursday 6th September)

The start of the Senior MGP event was delayed by an hour due to heavy rain in the morning, the course being slow to dry out once the rain had stopped and waiting for visibility to improve on the mountain. There were still damp patches around the course, especially between Parliament Square and The Waterworks section. The first rider away from a list of 97 competitors was G. Little (Moto Guzzi) at 11.45am. Alastair King (Norton) again made a lightning start and by the end of the first lap he was 17sec ahead of second place man R.H.F. Anderson (Norton), and J. Buchan (Norton) in third. Bernard got a good start and was lying sixth. The positions after lap one were:

1st A. King (Norton) 25m 27.2sec, 88.98mph
2nd R.H.F. Anderson (Norton) 25m 44.2sec, 88.00mph
3rd J. Buchan (Norton) 25m 45sec, 87.95mph
4th W.A. Holmes (Norton) 26m 03.8sec, 86.88mph
5th R. Dowty (Norton) 26m 13sec, 86.38mph
6th B.D. Codd (Norton) 26m 13.6sec, 86.34mph

Speeds increased on the second lap, partly due to the track drying out and partly due to the riders getting into a rhythm. A. King improved his lap time by over 28sec but there was still only 10sec separating the first three riders. Bernard had passed Dowty and was now up to fifth place and going well. The leader board after lap two was:

1st A. King (Norton) 50m 26.2sec, 89.78mph
2nd R.H.F. Anderson (Norton) 50m 33sec, 89.58mph
3rd J. Buchan (Norton) 50m 35.6sec, 89.50mph
4th W.A. Holmes (Norton) 51m 27.6sec, 88.00mph
5th B.D. Codd (Norton) 51m 58.4sec, 87.12mph
6th E.M Haldane (Norton) 52m 05.8sec, 86.92mph

Alastair King, while still leading, crashed on the third lap at a still-slippery Ramsey Hairpin; he was uninjured, but he broke the rear brake rod on his Norton forcing him to retire in third position. This put Anderson in the lead as he came into the pits for his refuelling stop, which took 21sec. Buchan also stopped for fuel taking 29sec. Bernard, too, pitted on this lap and was the quickest of the leading riders taking only 20sec, a remarkable time in the day considering J. Drysdale who finished the race in ninth place took over a minute to refuel. Even though J. Buchan had stopped for fuel on lap three he posted the fastest lap so far with a time of 24m 38.4sec, which put him in first place 4.4sec ahead of Anderson. The lap three leader board was:

1st J. Buchan (Norton) 1h 15m 14sec, 90.28mph
2nd R.H.F. Anderson (Norton) 1h 15m 18.4sec, 90.19mph
3rd A. King (Norton) 1h 16m 28.6sec, 88.82mph
4th W.A. Holmes (Norton) 1h 16m 34.8sec, 88.70mph
5th B.D. Codd (Norton) 1h 17m 29.2sec, 87.65mph
6th E.M. Haldane (Norton) 1h 17m 32.6sec, 87.59mph

Bernard pulled into the pits and shouted to his pit crew that his clutch was slipping. They made some quick adjustments and Bernard was on his way again. It was later discovered that the mainshaft nut had worked its way loose and he retired on the fifth lap. The positions after lap four were:

1st J. Buchan (Norton) 1h 40m 34.4sec, 90.04mph
2nd R.H.F. Anderson (Norton) 1h 40m 40.2sec, 89.95mph
3rd W.A. Holmes (Norton) 1h 42m 02.2sec 88.75mph
4th = E.M. Haldane (Norton) & E.F.H. Boyce (Norton) 1h 43m 33sec, 87.46mph
6th E.B. Crooks (Norton) 1h 44m 02sec, 87.05mph

The contest for the lead continued into the fifth lap between Buchan and Anderson with Buchan pulling out a gap of 11.8sec by the end of the lap, which equated to a speed of 90.51mph. The positions after lap five were:

1st J. Buchan (Norton) 2h 05m 03.2sec, 90.51mph
2nd R.H.F. Anderson (Norton) 2h 05m 15sec, 90.38mph
3rd W.A. Holmes (Norton) 2h 06m 37.4sec, 89.39mph
4th E.F.H. Boyce (Norton) 2h 08m 24.6sec, 88.15mph
5th E.M. Haldane (Norton) 2h 08m 45.6sec, 87.91mph
6th E.B. Crooks (Norton) 2h 09m 01.2sec, 87.73mph

Anderson began his final lap not knowing how far he was behind Buchan as he had started the race 2m 20sec before Buchan, so it was a matter of putting in the quickest lap time he could and he did, posting his best time of the day and hoping for the best. Unfortunately, it wasn't quite quick enough, and Buchan crossed the line winning by just 3.2sec. The result was:

1st J. Buchan (Norton) 2h 29m 32.2sec, 90.83mph
2nd R.H.F. Anderson (Norton) 2h 29m 35.4sec, 90.80mph
3rd W.A. Holmes (Norton) 2h 30m 49.2sec, 90.06mph
4th E.F.H. Boyce (Norton) 2h 33m 12.8sec, 88.66mph
5th E.B. Crooks (Norton) 2h 33m 56.2sec, 88.24mph
6th R. Dowty (Norton) 2h 34m 01.8sec, 88.19mph

Fastest lap: W.A. Holmes (Norton) final lap, 24m 11.8sec, 93.59mph (new record)

As you can see from the results, Norton dominated this event as BSA had dominated the Clubmans event earlier in the season. The first two non-Nortons home were K.H. Patrick (BSA) in eleventh place and W.J. Sawford (Matchless) in twelfth. The first seventeen finishers received a Replica, and the Club Team prize was won by The Southern (Isle of Man) Team, which consisted of W.A. Holmes (Norton), E.B. Crooks (Norton) and R. Dowty (Norton). The Lady Hill Trophy presented for the best performance by a Manx rider was awarded to E.B. Crooks (Norton) who finished second in the Junior race and fifth in the Senior. Bernard's fastest lap of the race was his third lap of 25m 30.8sec.

CHAPTER SEVEN

SCARBOROUGH INTERNATIONAL

"Flying Farmer"

Oliver's Mount road circuit at Scarborough was the next meeting on the calendar. This three-day international meeting on 13th, 14th and 15th September, organised by The Scarborough & District Motor Club Ltd, attracted a record crowd. Thursday was a practice day with two sessions: one in the morning 9.00am - 12.00 noon and one in the afternoon 2.00pm - 5.00pm. The first of the races held on the Friday were the heats for the 250cc event. There were two eliminating heats run over six laps of the 2.4-mile circuit. P.H. Tait (Velocette) took the lead in heat one followed by M.P. O'Rourke (MV Agusta). On the second lap O'Rourke had taken the lead only to crash and retire at Mere Hairpin. D.V. Chadwick (MV Agusta), who had been third, passed Tait on the penultimate lap and went on to win relatively easily.

250cc Eliminating Heat One: (6 laps)
1st D.V. Chadwick (203cc MV Agusta) 14m 56sec £4.00
2nd P.H. Tait (249cc Velocette) £3.00
3rd A.A. Williams (248cc Moto- Guzzi) £3.00
4th T.E. Fenwick (248cc Moto-Guzzi)
5th G.J. Turner (249cc Rudge)
6th D. Whelan (248cc Velocette)

In heat two B. Purslow (NSU) took the lead from the start and pulled away from J. Buchan (Norton). On the last lap an oil pipe burst on his NSU, but he had a big enough lead that he could stop his engine and still coast across the line to win by over 20 seconds.

250cc Eliminating Heat Two: (6 laps)
1st B. Purslow (247cc NSU) 15m 22sec £4.00
2nd J. Buchan (246cc Norton) £3.00
3rd W.J. Maddrick (248cc Moto-Guzzi) £3.00
4th I.F. Telfer (247cc Norton)
5th T.E. Rutherford (248cc Rudge)
6th J. Eckart (249cc Excelsior)

The three eliminating heats for the 350cc event were run over eight laps and won by P.H. Carter (Norton), R. McIntyre (Norton) and P. Murphy (AJS).

350cc Eliminating Heat one (8 laps)
1st P.H. Carter (348cc Norton) 19m 03.8sec £5.00
2nd R. Anderson (349cc AJS) £4.00
3rd B.D. Codd (348cc Norton) £3.00
4th R. Fay (350cc AJS)
5th P. Ferbrache (AJS or Norton)
6th S.T. Barnett (348cc Norton)

350cc Eliminating Heat Two (8 laps)
1st R. McIntyre (348cc Norton) £5.00
2nd D.V. Chadwick (348cc Norton) £4.00
3rd B. Freestone (348cc Norton) £3.00
4th P.A. Davey (348cc BSA)
5th R. Cousins (348cc Norton)
6th J.A. Sugden (348cc BSA)

350cc Eliminating Heat Three (8 laps)
1st P. Murphy (348cc AJS) 18m 40.2sec £5.00
2nd A. King (348cc Norton) £4.00
3rd E.R. Fitton (348cc Velocette) £3.00
4th G.A. Catlin (348cc Norton)
5th E.M. Haldane (348cc BSA)
6th J.B. Denton (348cc BSA)

Then there were two eliminating heats for 500cc Sidecars, each run over five laps. The first heat was won by E. Strub (Norton) from Switzerland. Pip Harris (Norton) dropped back from second place to finish fourth after his Norton suffered with a slipping clutch. Stan Dibben was the passenger for Pip Harris after his regular passenger had lost his grip and fallen out of the outfit during one of the practice sessions on Thursday; thankfully he wasn't seriously injured. In heat two J. Drion and his female passenger I. Stoll won on a BMW outfit.

500cc Sidecar Eliminating Heat One (5 laps) clutch start
1st E. Strub / C. Hilmat (499cc Norton) £5.00

2nd P. Woollett / N.J. Candy (499cc Norton) £4.00
3rd C. Freeman / T. Leek, (499cc Norton) £3.00
4th P.V. Harris / S. Dibben (499cc Norton) £2.00

500cc Sidecar Eliminating Heat Two (5 laps)
1st J. Drion / I. Stoll (492cc BMW) 12m 44.8sec £5.00
2nd J. Beeton / L. Nutt or C. Billingham (499cc Norton) £4.00
3rd E. Walker / D.G. Roberts (499cc Norton) £3.00
4th J.W. Beevers / W.J. Mundy (499cc Norton) £2.00

The 350cc Scratch Race Final (comprising the 16 second-fastest finishers from the 350cc heats) was won by R.B. Rensen (Norton) after P.H. Tait had taken an early lead but then dropped back on lap five and could only finish fourth; H. Plews finished second with J.B. Denton (BSA) third. D. Whelan (AJS) M.J. Candy (Norton) E.M. Haldane (BSA) and K. Kay (BSA) all retired. The result was:

350cc Scratch Race Final (12 laps)
1st R.B. Rensen (349cc Norton) 59.70mph, £8.00
2nd H. Plews (349cc Norton) £6.00
3rd J.B. Denton (348cc BSA) £5.00
4th P.H. Tait (348cc AJS) £4.00
Fastest lap: P.H. Tait (348cc AJS) 2m 20sec, 62.06mph

The last race on Friday was the 350cc Junior Final run over 16 laps. Bernard started this race but there is no record of him in the results in the programme, although it doesn't say that he retired. R. McIntyre lead from start to finish with P. Murphy second.

350cc Junior Final (16 laps)
The Winner received the "News Chronicle" Junior Challenge Trophy, to be held from meeting to meeting or a maximum of one year.
1st R. McIntyre (348cc Norton) 62.41mph, £40.00 and Replica
2nd P. Murphy (348cc AJS), £33.00 and Replica
3rd D.V. Chadwick (348cc Norton) £26.00 and Replica
4th A. King (348cc Norton) £16.00 and Replica
5th B. Freestone (348cc Norton) £12.00 and Replica
Fastest lap: R. McIntyre (348cc Norton) 63.98mph

The first race on Saturday was the 250cc Lightweight Final, run over 12 laps and again composed of the 16 fastest finishers from the heats. D.V. Chadwick (MV Agusta) and B. Purslow (NSU) got a good start and pulled away from the rest of the field. Chadwick then left Purslow and won by 70sec. He had lapped 11 of the 16 starters and broke his own lap record with a time of 2m 23sec, a speed of 60.76mph.

250cc Lightweight Final (12 laps)
The Winner received the "News Chronicle" Lightweight Challenge Trophy to be held from meeting to meeting or a maximum of one year.
1st D.V. Chadwick (203cc MV Agusta) 29m 19.2sec, 59.27mph £23.00 and Replica
2nd B. Purslow (247cc NSU) £18.00 and Replica
3rd T.E. Fenwick (248cc Moto Guzzi) £15.00 and Replica
4th J. Buchan (246cc Norton) £10.00 and Replica
5th G.J. Turner (249cc Rudge) £8.00 and Replica
Fastest lap: D.V. Chadwick (203cc MV Agusta) 2m 23sec, 60.76mph (new lap record)

In eliminating Heat One of the 500cc event P.A. Davey (BSA) got off the line first but, by the end of the first lap, he was second behind R. McIntyre (Norton) with G. Catlin (Norton) third, closely followed by E.R. Fitton (Norton) who attempted an overtaking move on the bottom straight and lost control of his machine; he could not recover from a massive wobble and crashed. Even though he was travelling at over 100mph he escaped without serious injury, but the bike smashed through a wooden gate. R. McIntyre's fastest lap was 64.36mph; Bernard was entered in this heat and came fourth. Geoff Duke (Gilera) won the second Heat by 25sec with A. King (Norton) second. Duke's fastest lap was 65.33mph riding the very fast and loud four-cylinder Gilera. R. Anderson (Norton) won the third Heat.

500cc Solo Eliminating Heat One (8 laps)
1st R. McIntyre (499cc Norton) £5.00
2nd P.A. Davey (499cc BSA) £4.00
3rd G.A. Catlin (499cc Norton) £3.00
4th B.D. Codd (499cc Norton)

500cc Solo Eliminating Heat Two (8 laps)
1st G.E. Duke (493cc Gilera) 18m 6.4sec £5.00

2nd A. King (499cc Norton) 18m 14.6sec £4.00
3rd P. Murphy (498cc Matchless) 18m 56sec £3.00
4th F. Purslow (499cc Norton) 18m 57.4sec
5th G. Tanner (500cc Norton)
6th H. Plews (499cc Norton)

500cc Solo Eliminating Heat Three (8 laps)
1st R. Anderson (499cc Norton) £5.00
2nd T.S Shepherd (499cc Norton) £4.00
3rd G.T. Salt (499cc Norton) £3.00
4th P.H. Carter (499cc Norton)
5th F. Wallis (498cc Matchless)

The 500cc Sidecar Final was run over seven laps and was composed of the eight fastest finishers from the two Sidecar Heats. Pip Harris (499cc Norton) started from the back row of the grid as he had been ninth fastest in his Heat the previous day, but F. Pusey (498cc BSA) was unable to start the race, so Harris was first reserve. J. Drion (492cc BMW) got a good start and was still leading at the end of lap one, followed by E. Strub (499cc Norton). Pip Harris charged his way through the field to fourth place and by lap four had taken the lead. The lead didn't last for long though; his Norton stopped as he approached Memorial Corner due to a blocked carburettor and by the time the problem had cleared itself and power was restored to his motor, he had been passed by four outfits. He managed to get back one place but the best he could finish was fourth. The result was:

500cc Sidecar Final (7 laps)
The Winner received the "News Chronicle" Sidecar Challenge Trophy to be held from meeting to meeting or a maximum of one year.
1st J. Drion / I. Stoll (492cc BMW) 57.46mph £25.00 and Replica
2nd E. Strub / Cecco Hilmat (499cc Norton) £20.00 and Replica
3rd J. Beeton / L. Nutt or C. Billingham (499cc Norton) £15.00 and Replica
4th P.V. Harris / R. Campbell (499cc Norton) £10.00 and Replica
5th E. Walker / D. Roberts (499cc Norton) £8.00 and Replica
Fastest lap: P.V. Harris (499cc Norton) 59.35mph

The penultimate race of the weekend was the Scratch race for 350cc or 500cc machines composing of the 16 second fastest finishers from the 500cc Heats.

350cc or 500cc Solo Scratch Race (12 laps)
1st B. Freestone (499cc Norton) 63mph £10.00
2nd P. Ferbrache (498cc Norton) £8.00
3rd J. Eckart (499cc Norton) £6.00
4th R. Fay (500cc Norton) £5.00
5th L. Carr (498cc Matchless) £4.00
Fastest lap: B. Freestone (499cc Norton) 64.47mph

The 500cc Final was started by Ingeborg Stoll, the female sidecar passenger of Jacques Drion. Bob McIntyre led Geoff Duke for the first three laps but then Duke took the lead and the pair of them were in a race of their own and soon half a minute ahead of the rest. For most of the race they battled wheel to wheel but the superiority of the Gilera showed in the end and Duke finished 7 seconds ahead of McIntyre. Duke's fastest lap was 2mph slower than his own lap record.

On the lap of honour Duke and McIntyre swapped machines, which caused some confusion for the officials, but it showed the friendship that existed in their rivalry back in the 'good old days' of motor sport. Unfortunately, it looks as though Bernard didn't finish the race in the Final of the 500cc event, but when he retired and why, I can't discover.

500cc Solo Final (16 laps)
The Winner received the "News Chronicle" Gold Challenge Trophy to be held from meeting to meeting or a maximum of one year.
1st G.E. Duke (493cc Gilera) 66.00mph £50.00 and Replica
2nd R. McIntyre (499cc Norton) £40.00 and Replica
3rd R. Anderson (499cc Norton) £30.00 and Replica
4th T.S. Shepherd (499cc Norton) £20.00 and Replica
5th P.A. Davey (499 BSA) £15.00 and Replica

There were also special awards given for the fastest lap in each class (£3.00), an award for the Course lap record (£5.00), and the Feridax Trophy (presented by Jim Feriday). The prizegiving was held on Saturday 15th at the Olympia Ballroom, Scarborough.

It is not known if Bernard travelled home on the Saturday night or early Sunday morning but he and many of the other riders who attended the three-day meeting at Oliver's Mount were at Cadwell Park the following day, 16th

September, for what turned out to be a record-breaking day's racing in conditions that were described as perfect. The start of the programme was delayed slightly as riders not only had to travel from Scarborough, but they also needed time to set their machines up for the Cadwell Park circuit. Bernard was one rider with this problem. He had not been happy with the 350cc Norton that he rode at Oliver's Mount so it was decided they would collect his old 350cc machine from Sam Coupland's workshop at Frithville on the Sunday morning. This they did and somehow managed to get the bike set up and prepared in time for the start of racing.

Bernard had the luxury of knowing that he could not be caught in the 350cc class as he had scored a maximum of 32 points in the series so far, winning the previous four rounds at the Easter, Whit, July, and August Bank Holiday meetings. His closest rivals were B. Freestone on 17 points, and G. Catlin and K.H. Patrick on 15 points. Bernard therefore won the Hammond Trophy for the 350cc Solo class.

The racing began with the under 50cc class. This was the first time this event had been held at Cadwell Park and, with machines of such a small capacity and Cadwell with all its undulations, was a very challenging track. It stated in the programme that *"One of these* [flyweights] *with rider is equivalent to one senior machine carrying nine other motorcycles and ten men".*

E. Penden (49cc NSU Quickly) led after the first lap with J.C. Hennett (49cc Itom Astor) second and G.L. Bird (48cc Itom Sport) third; R.R. Dendy was fourth on his streamlined Ducati. Penden continued to extend his lead throughout the race and won by a convincing 17 seconds. Bird and Dendy passed Hennett to finish second and third respectively.

50cc Flyweight Championship (3 laps)
1st E. Penden (49cc NSU Quickly) 5m 57.4sec, 37.8mph, £4.00
2nd G.L. Bird (48cc Itom Sport) £3.00
3rd R.R. Dendy (49cc Dendy Ducati) £2.00

The next race was the Lightweight Championship for Solo machines under 250cc. Bob McIntyre was making his first appearance at Cadwell Park and showed what a quality rider he was: he not only won the 250cc Lightweight event but in doing so he shattered the lap record by 11.2 seconds. The previous record of 10m 36.6sec had been held by John Surtees (248cc R.E.G.) since July

1954. (R.E.G.s were specials built, and sometimes ridden, by R.E. Geeson). The result was:

250cc Lightweight Championship (8 laps)
1st R. McIntyre (249cc Norton) 10m 25.4sec, 57.5mph £10.00
2nd P.H. Tait (248cc Beasley Velocette) £7.00
3rd G.A. Catlin (249cc NSU) £4.00
4th T.E. Fenwick (248cc Moto-Guzzi) £3.00

In the first heat of the 350cc Junior Championship J. Hartle beat Bernard's previous lap record of 7m 33.4sec by 2.6 seconds, but Bernard on his old 348cc Norton took back the record in the next heat with a time of 7m 25sec. The final of this event saw Peter Murphy from Australia on a works AJS (also on his first visit to Cadwell Park) taking the lead from the start, followed by the Nortons of Bernard and Bob McIntyre, the three riders all lapping consistently throughout the race. John Hartle (348cc Norton) caught and passed George Catlin (348cc Norton) to take fourth place, but he was unable to make up any ground on the leading three. Bernard attempted an overtaking move on Murphy on the exit of Barn Corner on the final lap, but this was unsuccessful, and he finished just 6 tenths of a second behind the Australian but well ahead of McIntyre. The result was:

350cc Junior Championship Final (8 laps)
1st P. Murphy (348cc AJS) 9m 46sec, 61.5mph £20.00
2nd B.D. Codd (348cc Norton) £12.00
3rd R. McIntyre (348cc Norton) 10.00
4th J. Hartle (348cc Norton) £5.00

The Standard reported this meeting in the Saturday 22nd September issue and in this article, I found the first reference to Bernard being called the "Flying Farmer". The reporter went on to mention the quality of opposition Bernard had been racing against and beaten in his first full season of Road Racing: riders such as John Surtees, Bob McIntyre, John Hartle and Derek Minter; all riders who would become world famous in the sport of motorcycle racing.

Bob McIntyre and John Hartle both showed their quality in the final of the Senior Championship event. Hartle led at the end of the first lap and was determined to keep McIntyre behind him. On the seventeenth lap Hartle used the superior speed of his Norton on the straight to pull away from McIntyre. He crossed the line to win by 6.2 seconds. A. Trow (499cc Norton) finished third with P. Ferbrache (499cc Norton) fourth. Bernard finished a very creditable fifth in front of P. Davey (499cc BSA). The result was:

Senior Championship (20 laps)

1st J. Hartle (499cc Norton) 23m 33.4sec, 63.6mph £40.00
2nd R. McIntyre (499cc Norton) £30.00
3rd A.J. Trow (499cc Norton) £20.00
4th P. Ferbrache (499cc Norton) £10.00
5th B.D. Codd (499cc Norton) £5.00
6th P.A. Davey (499cc BSA) £3.00

John Hartle's best lap was 1m 8.8sec, an average of 66mph. His time at the end of eight laps was 9m 36sec, 62.5mph, and in achieving this time he won the "Folbigg Trophy" for recording the fastest eight laps of the year. The previous best recorded time was George Catlin's 9m 48sec, which he set on 6th August.

P.V. (Pip) Harris (499cc Norton) was dominant in the Sidecar events, winning both the Championship and Handicap finals. In the Championship event he started well and stayed in front until the end, also shattering his own lap record by three seconds. He was followed home by W.G. Boddice (499cc Norton) and F. Taylor (499ccNorton). Starting from the back of the grid in the Handicap race Harris passed F. Hanks (499cc Norton) on the last lap to claim his second victory of the day. The results were:

Sidecar Championship Final (20 laps)

1st P.V. Harris / R. Campbell (499cc Norton) 10m 20.6sec, 57.1mph (new record) £40.00
2nd W.G. Boddice / W. Storr (499cc Norton) £30.00
3rd F. Taylor / R. Taylor (499cc Norton) £20.00
4th J. Beeton / C. Billingham (499cc Norton) £10.00

Sidecar Handicap Final (8 laps)

1st P.V. Harris / R. Campbell (499cc Norton) 11m 37.4sec, 51.8mph £15.00
2nd F. Hanks / E. Dorman (498cc Matchless) £10.00
3rd O.E. Greenwood / Unknown (499cc Norton) £8.00
4th W.G. Boddice / W. Storr (499cc Norton) £5.00

Vintage Championship for machines over 25 years old (8 laps)
1st H.D. German (1927, 348cc Velocette) 10m 44.6sec, 55.6mph £8.00
2nd B. Fowler (1930, 499cc Sunbeam) £6.00
3rd J.H. Diver (1925, 490cc Norton) £4.00

The Bascomb Trophy was also decided at this meeting, being awarded to the rider who had accumulated the most points throughout the season in all combined Solo classes. Going into this meeting the points table was:

1st B.D. Codd 54 points
2nd G.A. Catlin 52 points
3rd = B. Freestone and J. Eckart 30 points

George Catlin had the chance to win a possible 21 points as he was entered in the Junior and Senior on his Nortons, and the Lightweight class on an NSU. Bernard only had the opportunity to gain 16 more points as he was only entered in the Junior and Senior events. There were points awarded for the Heats as well as the Finals but there is no record that I can find of these results. The only thing that can be said with any certainty is that Bernard scored at least one second place in the 350cc Final and a fifth place in the Senior Championship Final. George, as far as I can see, only scored a third place in the 250cc Lightweight Championship Final and a fifth place in his 350cc Heat. So, I am assuming Bernard won the Bascomb Trophy as well as the Hammond Trophy at this meeting, but I will research this further.

Saturday September 22nd and the B.M.C.R.C. (British Motorcycle Racing Club) International Hutchinson"100" Meeting at Silverstone. The conditions were perfect for racing with warm bright sunshine throughout the day. The first race of the day started at 10.15am and was the 175cc to 250cc ten-lap event.

C. Sandford (250cc F.B. Mondial) had an easy victory, being able to use the superior power of his machine on the fast Silverstone circuit. Bob McIntyre (246cc Norton) had a fierce battle with M.P. O'Rourke (203cc MV Agusta) for second place. Even though O'Rourke had been last away from the line he managed to fight his way to third place and into the slipstream of McIntyre by lap six, but McIntyre held second place riding the impressive Joe Potts Norton and finished 15 seconds ahead of O'Rourke.

250cc Solo Race (10 laps)

1st C.C. Sandford (250cc F.B. Mondial) 20m 24sec, 85.89mph

2nd R. McIntyre (246cc Norton)

3rd M.P. O'Rourke (203cc MV Agusta)

Fastest lap: C.C. Sandford (250cc F.B. Mondial) 1m 59.8sec, 87.76mph

Bernard was entered in the first of two preliminary 350cc races and was involved in an epic battle for second place with J.R. Clark (349cc Arter AJS), J. Storr (349cc Norton), A. Trow (348cc Norton), F. Perris (349cc AJS) and A. Rutherford (348cc BSA). Jack Brett (348cc Norton) pulled out a lead and won, leaving the other six riders to fight it out for the runner-up spot. Each lap, they swapped positions in an exhilarating contest that lasted right to the chequered flag, and Clark just beat Trow by half a bikes length. Unfortunately, the report doesn't state where Bernard finished but there was only 1.8 seconds separating second placed Clark from seventh place, so Bernard was not that far behind them.

There was a three-rider battle in the second of the 350cc races involving J. Hartle, R. McIntyre and Alastair King, all on 348cc Nortons. Hartle won, with McIntyre second and King third, less than a second behind the winner.

First 350cc Solo Race (5 laps)

Fastest 48 riders to finish in the two 350cc Heats qualified for the Final

1st J. Brett (348cc Norton) 9m 59.8sec, 87.64mph

2nd J.R. Clark (349cc Arter AJS)

3rd J.A. Storr (349cc Norton)

Fastest lap: J. Brett (348cc Norton) 1m 57.6sec, 89.40mph

Second 350cc Solo Race (5 laps)

1st J. Hartle (348cc Norton) 9m 57.4sec, 87.99mph

2nd R. McIntyre (348cc Norton)

3rd A. King (348cc Norton)

Fastest lap J. Hartle (348cc Norton) 1m 56.6sec, 90.17mph

There was another hard-fought contest in the first 500cc race between R. Anderson (499cc Norton), F. Perris (498cc Matchless), J. Brett (499cc Norton), J.A. Storr (499cc Norton) and A. Trow (499cc Norton). Brett came out the winner but again there was very little separating the first five. R. McIntyre

(499cc Norton) comfortably won the second 500cc Race with T.S. Shepherd (499cc Norton) finishing second.

First 500cc Solo Race (5 laps)
Fastest 48 riders to finish in the two 500cc Heats qualified for the Final
1st J. Brett (499cc Norton) 9m 35.6sec, 91.33mph
2nd R.H.F. Anderson (499cc Norton)
3rd F.G. Perris (498cc Matchless)
Fastest lap: A.J. Trow (499cc Norton) 1m 50.8sec, 94.89mph

Second 500cc Solo Race (5 laps)
1st R. McIntyre (499cc Norton) 9m 45.2sec, 89.83mph
2nd T.S. Shepherd (499cc Norton)
3rd R.N. Brown (Matchless)
Fastest lap: R. McIntyre (499cc Norton) 1m 53.8sec, 92.38mph

Sidecar Race (10 laps)
1st P.V. Harris / R. Campbell (499cc Norton), 20m 33sec, 85.27mph
2nd C. Smith / S. Dibben (499cc Norton/Watsonian)
3rd J. Beeton / C. Billingham (499cc Norton/Watsonian)
Fastest lap: P.V. Harris (499cc Norton) 2m 0.2sec, 87.47mph

C. Sandford won both the 125cc and 250cc Championship races relatively easily. Despite a poor start in the 125cc event he had a commanding lead after the first lap and won the race by nearly one minute. In the 250cc event he also had things his own way beating D.V. Chadwick (203cc MV Agusta) and R. McIntyre (246cc Norton). Sandford was so dominant in this race that he lapped every rider up to and including T. Shepherd (247cc Norton) in fourth place.

125cc Solo Championship Race (10 laps)
1st C.C. Sandford (125cc Mondial) 22m 20sec, 78.46mph
2nd W.J. Maddrick (124cc MV Agusta)
3rd A.F. Wheeler (123cc MV Agusta)
Fastest lap: C. Sandford (125cc Mondial) 2m 10.8sec, 80.38mph
(New Record)

250cc Solo Championship Race (20 laps)
1st C. Sandford (250cc Mondial) 41m 18.4sec, 84.81mph also won

(The Dunlop Trophy)
2nd D.V. Chadwick (203cc MV Agusta)
3rd R. McIntyre (246cc Norton)
Fastest lap: C. Sandford (250cc Mondial) 2m 1.4sec, 86.60mph

Bernard was on the front row of the grid for the 350cc Championship race alongside McIntyre, King, Brett, Hartle, Perris, Brown, and Shepherd. J. Brett took an early lead but as they started the second lap McIntyre was leading with Hartle second, Brett third and King fourth. This battle continued for 18 laps until Brett came over the line having passed McIntyre and Hartle and pulled a slight lead. He won by 4.8 seconds.

Bernard had a race-long battle with Shepherd, Trow, Brown, Clark and Storr for fifth place. They swapped places on each lap and were never more than a few feet apart racing at over 100mph. T.S. Shepherd eventually got the better of the others and finished fourth. Again, there was no mention of Bernard's final position.

350cc Solo Championship Race (20 laps)
1st J. Brett (348cc Norton) 38m 59.4sec, 89.88mph
(also won The Avon Trophy)
2nd R. McIntyre (348cc Norton)
3rd J. Hartle (348cc Norton)
Fastest lap: R. McIntyre (348cc Norton) 1m 55sec, 91.42mph

Jack Brett (499cc Norton) got a bad start in the 500cc Championship Race but battled his way through the field to finish third behind J. Hartle and R. McIntyre, also on Nortons. Bernard qualified for this race but unfortunately there is no mention of him in the results.

500cc Championship Race (20 laps)
1st J. Hartle (499cc Norton) 38m 3.4sec, 92.08mph
(also won The AMC Challenge Trophy)
2nd R. McIntyre (499cc Norton)
3rd J. Brett (499cc Norton)
Fastest lap: T.S. Shepherd (499cc Norton) 1m 51sec, 94.82mph

Sidecar Championship Race (12 laps)
1st P.V. Harris / R. Campbell (499cc Norton), 24m 39.2sec, 85.29mph

2nd C. Smith / S. Dibben (499cc Norton/Watsonian)
3rd J. Beeton / C. Billingham (499cc Norton/Watsonian)
Fastest lap: P.V. Harris (499cc Norton) 2m 0.4sec, 87.32mph

The Mellano (Hutchinson) Trophy was awarded to the rider whose average race speed exceeded the class lap record by the greatest margin or, if the lap record was not exceeded, it was awarded to the rider whose speed was the nearest to the lap record. It was awarded to C. Sandford (125cc Mondial) who, at 78.46mph, was 1.83mph faster than the previous 125cc lap record.

The George Reynolds Memorial Trophy was awarded to the rider with the fastest lap of the day, A.J. Trow (499cc Norton) 1m 50.8sec, 94.89mph.

Saturday 29th September was the day of the Blackburn Open-Centre Meeting at the 1.17-mile Brough Aerodrome Circuit. There was an unusually small crowd, which the organisers attributed to being the first Saturday Meeting at Brough. It was also extremely windy. Alastair King (Norton) won both the 350cc and 500cc Finals, but Bernard pushed him all the way in the 350cc Final when the two of them left the other riders to fight it out for third place.

Alastair King, George Catlin, and Brian Freestone (all on Nortons) won the 350cc Heats. King, Catlin, and R. Jervis (Nortons) won the 500cc Heats. In the Final of the 500cc race, George Catlin and Bernard got off to a good start but then Bernard hit the banking and broke his rear brake rod. He was able to stay in control of his Norton, but he had to retire. A. King and J.A. Storr (Norton) made their way up through the field to fight for the lead with Catlin. King reached the chequered flag first, lapping all but six of the other riders and just in front of J.A. Storr. George Catlin finished third. John Hartle, the Norton Works rider, was not able to attend due to National Service duties.

Pip Harris (Norton) regained the Sidecar lap record with a speed of 61.58mph, the previous record being held by C. Smith who posted a speed of 61.04mph in 1954. Harris then increased the record to 62.31mph in the Sidecar Handicap Final. The results were:

250cc Solo Final (7 laps)
1st T.E. Fenwick (Moto Guzzi) 56.37mph
2nd D. Whelan (Velocette)

3rd E.W. Tinkler (Moto Guzzi)
Fastest lap: T.E. Fenwick (Moto Guzzi) 58.83mph

350cc Solo Final (7 laps)
1st A. King (Norton) 63.43mph
2nd B.D. Codd (Norton)
3rd B. Freestone (Norton)
Fastest lap: A. King (Norton) 64.41mph

500cc Solo Final (20 laps)
1st A. King (Norton) 64.39mph
2nd J.A. Storr (Norton)
3rd G.A. Catlin (Norton)
Fastest lap: A. King (Norton) & G.A. Catlin (Norton) 65.81mph

Sidecar Scratch Final (7 laps)
1st P.V. Harris (Norton) 59.05mph
2nd J. Beeton (Norton)
3rd F. Taylor (Norton)
Fastest lap: P.V. Harris (Norton) 61.58mph

Sidecar Handicap Final (7 laps)
1st E. Walker (Norton) 57.95mph
2nd P.V. Harris (Norton)
3rd C. Freeman (Norton)
Fastest lap: P.V. Harris (Norton) 62.31mph (New Record)

Although there were three more meetings in the 1956 Road Racing Calendar - Crystal Palace on 6th October, Brands Hatch and Mallory Park on 7th October - I cannot find any record of Bernard attending these events in the reports or results, so I am assuming his season concluded at Brough Aerodrome. He did, however, participate in a Trials event, which was reported in the Louth Standard on Friday 7th December. This was the Grimsby Club's "BSA Sporting Cup Trial" held on 2nd December, and it was reported that Bernard had won it again for the fourth consecutive year. It also said in the report that he had won the Grantham Club's Trial the previous weekend. In both events he rode his 197cc James.

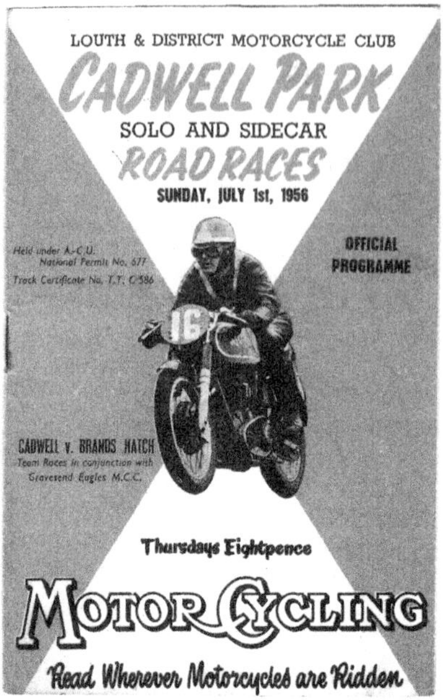

Cadwell Park programme
Sunday July 1st, 1956

Cadwell Park programme
August Bank Holiday Monday

Scarborough Int. programme
13th -15th September, 1956

Cadwell Park programme
Sunday 16th September, 1956

Cadwell Park advertisement for 1st July, 1956

Bernard leading Bob McIntyre in the 350cc final at Cadwell Park September 16th, 1956

Cadwell Park advertisement for Sunday 16th September, 1956

Silverstone programme
September 22nd, 1956

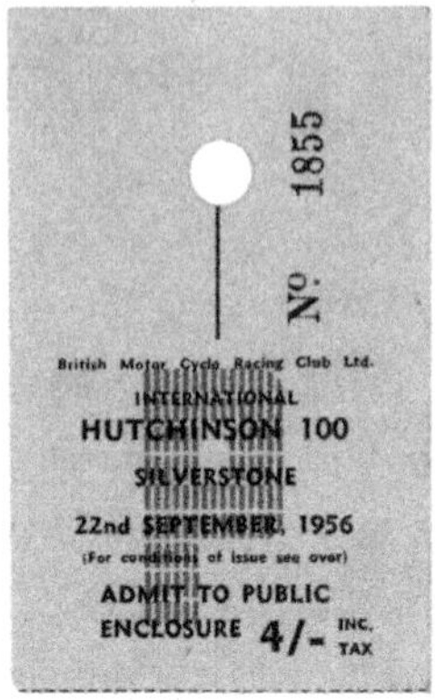

Bernard, Austin Munks and
Sam Coupland at the B.R.D.C
Civic Reception with Councillor A. Fyson

Bernard on the 350cc
Manx Norton
in the
Junior Manx Grand Prix 1956
on the Glencrutchery Road

Further on in the lap
of the Junior event

CHAPTER EIGHT

1957

"I feel sure that before long we shall see him get a works ride"

The Louth Standard reported on 25th January 1957 that The Lincoln MCC had awarded the "West Trophy" for the most meritorious performance in Road Racing in 1956 by a Club member to Bernard for his achievements in the Junior and Senior Clubman's TT.

The Cambridge Daily News, on 7th March 1957, published an article concerning the eminent local motorcycle dealers Hallens of Cambridge. Mr L.W. Hallen hosted a film show at the "Dorothy Café" to promote his motorcycle business to an audience of motorcycle enthusiasts, representatives of the trade and motorcycling press. The show was a "fly-on-the-wall" type documentary showing footage of recent scrambles events and local celebrities. Other films shown on the night were a production by Mobil Oil, which concentrated on recent record-breaking attempts by Donald Campbell on the World Water Speed Record in America, and a film by K.L.G (spark plug manufacturers), which gave a good report on activities in this country.

At the opening night of the show, Mr. Hallen introduced Bernard and a surprise item of news that the audience was not expecting: after two years of being sponsored by Austin Munks and Sam Coupland in Road Racing, and several years in Trials events prior to that, Bernard was going to be sponsored by Hallens of Cambridge for the 1957 season in National and International events. These would include the Isle of Man International TT and the North West 200. The reason for Munks and Coupland pulling out of sponsoring Bernard was given as *"Owing to business ties we feel unable to devote the necessary time this season to Codd's busy programme".* Bernard had already received his 500cc Manx Norton and was waiting for delivery of the 350cc model. Both were straight from the Norton factory. What an exciting prospect it must have been: a new sponsor, two new machines and a new season ahead.

The Newark Advertiser reported on Wednesday 13th March that the Newark Motorcycle & Light Car Club's Annual Dinner was held at the Robin Hood Hotel

Newark on Saturday 9th March, and they paid tribute to Bernard and his achievements in the previous year. Mr C.C. Cann proposed the toasts and welcomed Mr R. Clayton, the Chairman of the Lincoln Club. They both praised Bernard on his achievements. Mr Cann said, *"I feel sure that before long we shall see him get a works ride".*

Bernard's first competitive ride out on his two new Manx Nortons was at Mallory Park on 14th April. The meeting was an event organised by the Nottingham Tornado Club and had received a large entry.

T.S. Shepherd (MV Agusta) was dominant in the 250cc event. He won his heat with a fast time, and took an early lead in the final from B. Purslow (Streamlined NSU), T.E. Fenwick (Moto Guzzi), P. Tomes (JAP) and E.W. Tinkler (Velocette). The 250cc results were:

250cc Solo
Heat One
1st T.S. Shepherd (204cc MV Agusta) 4m 31sec, 79.67mph
2nd B. Purslow (247cc NSU) 4m 32.4sec
3rd W.A. Smith (250cc Excelsior) 4m 44sec
Heat Two
1st P. Tomes (248cc JAP) 4m 40.8sec
2nd T.E. Fenwick (248cc Moto Guzzi) 4m 41sec
3rd J. Patrick (248cc Velocette) 4m 41.4sec

Heat Three
1st F. Purslow (247cc NSU) 4m 38sec
2nd E.W. Tinkler (250cc KTT Velocette) 4m 38.6sec
3rd J.B. Elkington (250cc Rudge) 4m 39.4sec

250cc Final (6 laps)
1st T.S. Shepherd (204cc MV Agusta) 6m 33.2sec, 75mph
2nd B. Purslow (247cc NSU)
3rd T.E. Fenwick (248cc Moto Guzzi)
4th P. Tomes (248cc JAP)

There was such a large entry in the 350cc Solo class that they had to run seven preliminary heats with the fastest 20 qualifying for the Final. Bernard was in the second heat.

350cc Solo

Heat One

1st J.B. Denton (348cc BSA) 5m 6.2sec
2nd P.W. Read (348cc BSA) 5m 26.4sec
3rd F. Wallis (348cc BSA) 5m 27sec

Heat Two

1st P. Ferbrache (348cc Norton) 5m 16.6sec
2nd R. Anderson (348cc Norton) 5m 17.4sec
3rd B.D. Codd (350cc Norton) 5m 19sec

Heat Three

1st R. Fay (350cc AJS) 5m 29.8sec
2nd T. Phillipson (349cc AJS) 5m 30.6sec
3rd G.C.A. Murphy (348cc AJS) 5m 31.2sec

Heat Four

1st E. Hinton (350cc Norton)
2nd K.H. Patrick (350cc BSA)
3rd R.H. Lilley (350cc Norton)

Heat Five

1st H. Hinton (350cc Norton)
2nd R.S. Mayhew (348cc Velocette)
3rd L. Southam (348cc Norton) 5m 34.6sec

Heat Six

1st G. Downes (350cc AJS) 5m 35sec
2nd P. Tomes (248cc JAP) 5m 42.6sec
3rd E.W. Tinkler (250cc KTT Velocette) 5m 43.2sec

Heat Seven

1st J. Murgatroyd (248cc Beasley Velocette)

Unfortunately, the rest of the results for Heat Seven were not filled in on the programme, but as far as I can tell none of the competitors in this heat were in the fastest 20 in the event; therefore, none would have qualified for the Final.

Bernard was on the front row of the grid for the final of the 350cc event with P. Ferbrache (Norton), R. Anderson (Norton), the Hinton brothers (Eric and Harry) from Australia on Nortons and J.B. Denton (BSA). Terry Shepherd, who was hoping to repeat his earlier win in the 250cc race, was on the second row but his Norton was reluctant to start, and he was last away from the line. At the end of the first lap Bernard was leading with Denton and Ferbrache close behind. By the end of the next lap Ferbrache was in second place and was under pressure from Anderson. At the end of the fourth lap Anderson had taken the lead and Bernard had dropped down to fourth place where he finished. The result of the 350cc Final was:

350cc Solo Final (8 laps)

1st R. Anderson (348cc Norton) 8m 13.2sec, 78.83mph
2nd P. Ferbrache (348cc Norton) 8m 15.4sec
3rd E. Hinton (350cc Norton) 8m 15.6sec
4th B.D. Codd (350cc Norton) 8m 17sec

There were two heats in the Sidecar Scratch event, the first being won by A. Young (500cc Norton/Watsonian) who put up a phenomenal performance beating B. Boddice (499cc Norton) and C. Smith (499cc Norton). The second heat was won by O. Greenwood (499cc Norton).

Sidecar Scratch (5 laps)
Heat One

1st A. Young (500cc Norton/Watsonian) 5m 34sec
2nd B. Boddice (499cc Norton) 5m 36sec
3rd C. Smith (499cc Norton)

Heat Two

1st O. Greenwood (499cc Norton) 5m 42.4sec
2nd F. Taylor (499cc Norton/Watsonian) 5m 46.2sec
3rd K.A. Robinson (998cc Vincent Special) 5m 53.6sec
4th W. Evans (499cc Norton) 5m 54.4sec

In the final, B. Boddice led for the first two laps, but he was passed by C. Smith on lap three. A. Young, with the superior power of his 500cc Norton/Watsonian, passed them both and went on to win by two seconds.

Sidecar Scratch Final (8 laps)

1st A. Young (500cc Norton/Watsonian) 8m 46.6sec, 73.83mph
2nd C. Smith (499cc Norton) 8m 48.6sec
3rd W.G. Boddice (499cc Norton) 8m 52.8sec
4th F. Taylor (499cc Norton/Watsonian) 8m 53.6sec

There were six heats in the 500cc Solo Class with the fastest 20 qualifying for the final.

500cc Solo Heats (5 laps)

Heat One

1st E. Hinton (500cc Norton) 5m 07.4sec
2nd R. Fay (499cc Norton) 5m 19sec
3rd B. Purslow (499cc Norton) 5m 19.4sec

Heat Two

1st H. Hinton (500cc Norton)
2nd B.L. Denchy (499cc Norton)
3rd J.A. Sugden (348cc Norton)

Heat Three

1st R.S. Mayhew (499cc Norton) 5m 28sec
2nd P.W. Read (348cc BSA) 5m 29.6sec
3rd G. Bell (498cc Norton)

Heat Four

1st F. Wallis (499cc BSA) 5m 14.2sec
2nd K.H. Patrick (350cc BSA) 5m 19.8sec
3rd R.H. King (499cc Norton) 5m 33.4sec
4th G. Downes (350cc AJS)

Heat Five

1st S.A. Ward (499cc Norton) 5m 28.8sec
2nd B.J. Daniels (500cc BSA) 5m 30sec
3rd R. Watson (499cc Norton) 5m 32.4sec

Heat Six

1st F.A. Rutherford (499cc Duke BSA)
2nd N.H. Storer (499cc Norton JAP)
3rd R. Lawrence (350cc BSA)

Bernard was in heat one and, although he wasn't placed in the first three, he did qualify for the final. The Hinton brothers dominated the 500cc final finishing first and second with Fred Wallis third after he had led for the first three laps on what seemed a very quick BSA. F.A. Rutherford was fourth and Roy Jervis fifth. The result was:

500cc Solo Final (8 laps)
1st E. Hinton (500cc Norton) 80.83mph
2nd H. Hinton (500cc Norton)
3rd F. Wallis (499cc BSA)
4th F.A. Rutherford (499cc Duke BSA)
5th R. Jervis (499cc Norton)

Sidecar Handicap Heats (5 laps)
First six in each heat qualified for the final

Heat One
1st T. Folwell (498cc Matchless) 6m 23.2sec
2nd L. Wells (499cc Norton) 6m 24.8sec
3rd P.E.W. Russell (499cc Norton)
4th A. Young (500cc Norton/Watsonian)

Heat Two
1st D.H. Saywood (499cc Norton)
2nd F. Hanks (499cc Norton)
3rd F. Taylor (499cc Norton/Watsonian)

Sidecar Handicap Final (8 laps)
1st F. Hanks (499cc Norton) 72.5mph
2nd F. Taylor (499cc Norton/Watsonian)
3rd D.H. Saywood (499cc Norton)

Bernard was in heat one of the Unlimited cc classes but again, unfortunately, the results have not been filled in for the heats and there is no mention of him in any race reports so I can't say where he finished or even if he qualified for the final.

Unlimited cc Solo Class Heats (5 laps)
Heat One
1st H. Hinton (500cc Norton)

Heat Two
1st R. Jervis (499cc Norton)

Heat Three
1st A.J. Trow (499cc Norton)

Heat Four
1st R. Fay (499cc Norton)

Unlimited cc Solo Final (12 laps)
1st E. Hinton (500cc Norton) 83.76mph
2nd T.S. Shepherd (500cc Norton)
3rd H. Hinton (500cc Norton)

The next meeting was at Snetterton on Sunday 21st April and organised by "The Snetterton Combine" (Comprising the motorcycle clubs in Norfolk and Suffolk affiliated to the Eastern Centre of the ACU). There is very little in the way of a report for this meeting, but we do have the results:

125cc Race (4 laps)
1st D.H. Edlin (125cc MV Agusta) 66.74mph
2nd W. Peden (125cc NSU)
3rd J. Dakin (124cc EMC)
Fastest lap: D.H. Edlin (125cc MV Agusta) 68.06mph

The lap record in the 125cc class was held by John Hogan (125cc MV Agusta) at 71.37mph

250cc Race (6 laps)
1st G.E. Monty (250cc GMS MK 2) 75.06mph
2nd D.H. Edlin (250cc EMC)
3rd J. Murgatroyd (248cc Beasley Velocette)
Fastest lap: G.E. Monty (250cc GMS MK 2) 76.89mph

The lap record for the 250cc class of 80.86mph was held by John Surtees (250cc MV Agusta). The first heat of the 350cc event was won by P. Ferbrache (350cc Norton) with B.P. Setchell (350cc Norton) second and G. Tanner (350cc Norton) third.

350cc Solo Heats (7 laps)

Heat One
First 10 Finishers to qualified for the Final
1st P. Ferbrache (350cc Norton) 79.04mph
2nd B.P. Setchell (350cc Norton)
3rd G. Tanner (350cc Norton)

In heat two of the 350cc event Bernard did lead R. Anderson for a short time but Anderson passed him to take the win.

Heat Two
First 10 finishers to qualified for the Final
1st R. Anderson (350cc Norton)

In the final of the 350cc event Bernard again led for a short time but was passed and beaten by Anderson with G.B. Tanner (350cc Norton) third.

350cc Solo Final (10 laps)
1st R. Anderson (350cc Norton) 81.82mph
2nd B.D. Codd (350cc Norton)
3rd G.B. Tanner (350cc Norton)
Fastest lap G.C.A. Murphy (AJS) 82.37mph
The lap record for the 350cc Class was held by R. McIntyre (350cc Norton) 83.37mph

First Sidecar Race up to 500cc (6 laps)
1st P.V. Harris / R. Campbell (499cc Norton) 79.54mph
2nd J. Beeton / C. Billingham (499cc Norton/Watsonian)
3rd O.E. Greenwood / T. Fairbrother (499cc Norton)
Fastest lap: P.V. Harris (499cc Norton) 79.54mph
The lap record for the 500cc Sidecar Class was held by P.V. Harris (498cc Norton) 81.26mph

Second Sidecar Race up to 1200cc (6 laps)
1st P.V. Harris / R. Campbell (499cc Norton) 78.28mph
2nd J. Beeton / C. Billingham (499cc Norton/Watsonian)
3rd C. Smith / E. Bliss (499cc Norton/Watsonian)
Fastest lap: P.V. Harris (499cc Norton) 80.72mph

The lap record for the 1200cc Sidecar Class was held by P.V. Harris
(498cc Norton) 81.26mph

500cc Solo Heats (7 laps)
First 10 finishers in both heats qualified for the final

Heat One
1st D.G. Chapman (500cc Norton) 82.55mph

Heat Two
1st E. Minihan (500cc Norton) 81.12mph

500cc Solo Final (10 laps)
1st R. Anderson (500cc Norton) 84.67mph
2nd J. Lewis (499cc Norton)
3rd P. Ferbrache (500cc Norton)
Fastest lap: G.B. Tanner (500cc Norton) 86.33mph
The lap record for the 500cc Class was held by John Surtees
(500cc MV Agusta) 88.37mph

In the programme for this meeting there was a Miss P. Harman listed as a competitor riding a 348cc BSA-Norton. She worked as a telephonist at the ACU headquarters and was recently engaged to be married to Geoff Tanner, the Norton rider. This was to be her first race and it had caused a lot of controversy amongst the organisers. It turned out not to be a problem, however, because, apparently, when she tried to fit into her leathers, they were too tight and there were no others she could borrow so her racing debut had to be postponed.

The following day, Easter Monday 22nd April, at Oulton Park Bernard made a good start to the day by winning his heat of the 350cc event. The first Heat was won by John Hartle with Alastair King second. Unfortunately, a lot of the scribbling in the programme is unreadable and has obviously been hurried so I haven't included all the speeds as I can't be certain of their accuracy.

251cc -350cc Heats (5 laps)
Heat One
The first 16 riders qualified for the final
1st J. Hartle (348cc Norton) 78.34mph

2nd A. King (348cc Norton)
3rd T.S. Shepherd (349cc Norton)
4th R. Fay (348cc AJS)

251cc -350cc Heat Two
The first 16 riders qualified for the final
1st B.D. Codd (348cc Norton) 76.63mph
2nd A. Shepherd (348cc Norton)
3rd W.A. Holmes (348cc Norton)
4th M.T. Brookes (349cc Norton)

The 350cc Final was dominated by J. Hartle on his streamlined Norton, where he clearly had the speed advantage over Alastair King and Shepherd on naked Nortons. The three of them battled for the first five laps but then lost ground quickly, leaving Hartle out on his own. Bernard contested fourth place with Alan Holmes (348cc Norton) for most of the race but was able to keep in front of him and even take a well-earned third place when Shepherd suffered with gearbox trouble on the penultimate lap.

350cc Final (19 laps)
1st J. Hartle (348cc Norton) 79.2mph
2nd A. King (348cc Norton)
3rd B.D. Codd (348cc Norton)
Fastest lap J. Hartle (348cc Norton) 80.42mph

In the 150cc Solo Race C.C. Sandford (125cc FB Mondial) clearly had the advantage over the rest of the field increasing his lead by five seconds each lap and, in doing so, increased the previous lap record (which he had held at 70.39mph, 2m 21.2sec since 21st May 1956) by 6.2sec, almost 3mph faster. Second and third was D.V. Chadwick and D.H. Edlin both on MV Agustas.

150cc Solo Race (6 laps)
1st C.C. Sandford (125cc FB Mondial) 72.13mph
2nd D.V. Chadwick (123cc MV Agusta)
3rd D.H. Edlin (123cc MV Agusta)
4th W.M. Webster (123cc MV Agusta)
5th J. Hogan (123cc MV Agusta)
Fastest lap: C.C. Sandford (125cc FB Mondial) 73.3mph

Sandford also won the 250cc Race riding his 250cc Mondial, but he didn't dominate this race as he had done the 125cc event. John Surtees (203cc MV Agusta) led until he apparently hit a false neutral and crashed at "Cascades" bend. This left Sandford in the lead but followed by J. Hartle on the twin cylinder 248cc R.E.G. The battle for third place was contested between T. Shepherd on a naked 203cc MV Agusta and Sammy Miller on a streamlined NSU. Although Miller had the speed advantage on the straight, Shepherd gained time with superior corner speed and eventually finished in third place.

250cc Solo Race (6 laps)
1st C.C. Sandford (250cc FB Mondial) 76.17mph
2nd J. Hartle (248cc R.E.G.)
3rd T.S. Shepherd (203cc MV Agusta)
Fastest lap: J. Hartle (248cc R.E.G.) 77.17mph

The first Sidecar race was won by P.V. Harris (499cc Norton) who led from start to finish, but he was chased all the way to the chequered flag by C. Smith (499cc Norton/Watsonian) who repeatedly tried to overtake on the bends but couldn't find a way past. He did, however, post the fastest lap in trying. Bill Boddice (499cc Norton/Watsonian) finished third but could not match the pace of the leading two. E. Walker (499cc Norton) took advantage of J. Beeton's misfortune (his streamline fairing came loose) to finish fourth.

Sidecar Scratch Race One up to 1200cc (5 laps)
1st P.V. Harris / R. Campbell (499cc Norton) 75.3mph
2nd C. Smith / E. Bliss (499cc Norton/Watsonian)
3rd W.G. Boddice / B. Canning (499cc Norton/Watsonian)
4th E. Walker / D.G. Roberts (499cc Norton)
5th L.W. Taylor / P. Glover (499cc Norton)
6th F. Taylor / B. Simpson (499cc Norton/Watsonian)

In the second Sidecar Scratch race P.V. Harris (499cc Norton) was again the winner. C. Smith (499cc Norton/Watsonian) had a problem with a loose fuel pipe and couldn't match the pace of Harris this time, so Harris crossed the line 7 seconds ahead.

Sidecar Scratch Race Two up to 1200cc (5 laps)
1st P.V. Harris / R. Campbell (499cc Norton) 75.74mph
2nd C. Smith / E. Bliss (499cc Norton/Watsonian)

3rd J. Beeton / C. Billingham (499cc Norton/Watsonian)
Fastest lap: P.V. Harris (499cc Norton) 77.29mph

Cyril Smith had the consolation of winning the Sidecar Handicap race by passing F. Taylor (499cc Norton/Watsonian) on the last lap. J. Beeton was third.

Sidecar Handicap Race up to 1200cc (5 laps)
1st C. Smith / E. Bliss (499cc Norton/Watsonian) 75.19mph
2nd F. Taylor / B. Simpson (499cc Norton/Watsonian)
3rd J. Beeton / C. Billingham (499cc Norton/Watsonian)
Fastest lap: C. Smith (499cc Norton/Watsonian) 76.93mph

Heat one of the 500cc event was won by J. Surtees (499cc MV Agusta) with an average speed of 81.47mph. Bernard was entered in heat two of this event riding his 499cc Norton but there is no mention of him in the results or report of the race and he was not in the programme as one of the 32 starters for the final. Heat two was won by W.A. Holmes (499cc Norton) with an average speed of 76.21mph

In the final, Terry Shepherd (499cc Norton) fought hard with John Surtees on the four-cylinder 499cc MV Agusta, with them dicing for the lead until five laps from the end when Surtees had to retire with gearbox trouble. Shepherd lapped all other riders up to fifth place and posted the fastest lap of the day at 85.1mph, which was only eight-tenths of a second outside Geoff Duke's record set on the Gilera. R. Fay (499cc Norton) finished third.

500cc Solo Final (19 laps)
1st T.S. Shepherd (499cc Norton) 83.13mph
2nd J. Hartle (499cc Norton)
3rd R. Fay (499cc Norton)
4th W.A. Holmes (499cc Norton)
Fastest lap: T.S. Shepherd (499cc Norton) 85.1mph

As a point of interest, listed in the names of competitors at the front of the programme is a certain S.M.B. Hailwood from Henley-on-Thames. This was the first race meeting Mike Hailwood had competed in, just three weeks after his 17th birthday and, although this must have been an unnerving experience for him, it would soon be clear to see that he was a natural, and many believe him to be the greatest motorcycle racer of all time.

He was second reserve in the 150cc race riding a 123cc MV Agusta and after a dreadful start he settled down and finished eleventh. He again was second reserve in the 250cc event riding a 172cc MV Agusta. There is no mention of him getting the opportunity to compete in this race.

There was a meeting at Cadwell Park on the same day, but Bernard chose to race at Oulton Park instead, although the reason for this is unknown. The Cadwell Park meeting was well attended with over 120 entries which included George Catlin riding a pair of ex-John Surtees Nortons in the 350cc and 500cc events and an ex-Carlo Ubbiali MV Agusta in the 250cc class. This was the machine Ubbiali had raced in the 1956 International TT. Other solo entries included Fred Wallis, Peter Davy, Brian Freestone, Roy Jervis, and Ken Patrick. Sidecar entries included Owen Greenwood, Fred Hanks, John Harris, Bob Freeman, and Eric Cheney. Many of the competitors had spent the winter months tuning and preparing their machines for the start of the 1957 season. Phil Tait of Coventry was sponsored by Ernie Earls (the famous fork designer) and was competing on two Nortons and a very special 250cc twin cylinder J.E.L. machine which in tests had shown it was capable of a staggering top speed of over 115mph. The sidecar teams had been busy fabricating new streamlined bodies in aluminium and fibreglass for their outfits.

One-week later, on Saturday 27th April, Bernard was at the 1.84-mile-long Castle Combe Circuit near Bristol for a National Road Race Meeting organised by the Wessex Centre A.C.U.

MV Agustas dominated the 125cc race, occupying the top four places, with M.P. O'Rourke taking the win from D.H. Edlin, S. Rees, and S.M.B. Hailwood (who finished fourth in only his second time out).

125cc Solo Race (5 laps)
1st M.P. O'Rourke (MV Agusta) 67.51mph
2nd D.H. Edlin (MV Agusta)
3rd S. Rees (MV Agusta)
4th S.M.B. Hailwood (MV Agusta)
Fastest lap: M.P. O'Rourke (MV Agusta) 69.86mph (new lap record)

350cc Non- Experts Solo Race (6 laps)
1st L.S. Rutherford (AJS) 74.61mph
2nd J.R. Fordham (Norton)

3rd W.D. Craig (Norton)
Fastest lap: J.R. Fordham (Norton) 77.55mph

In the 250cc race M.P. O'Rourke (MV Agusta) finished first by a substantial distance from J.R. Clarke (Norton) in second place and J. Murgatroyd (Beasley Velocette) third. Mike Hailwood finished sixth out of a starting lineup of 32 on a 175cc MV Agusta.

250cc Solo Race (6 laps)
1st M.P. O'Rourke (MV Agusta) 72.97mph
2nd J.R. Clarke (Norton)
3rd J. Murgatroyd (Beasley Velocette)
Fastest lap: M.P. O'Rourke (MV Agusta) 75.61mph

Cyril Smith (Norton/Watsonian) won the Sidecar event but was pushed all the way by R. Robinson (Vincent Special) with W. Boddice (Norton/Watsonian) third. Robinson shattered the previous lap record with a speed of 78.66mph. The previous record was held by W. Boddice with a speed of 76.5mph.

Sidecar Scratch race (7 laps)
1st C. Smith / E. Bliss (Norton/Watsonian) 76.2mph
2nd R. Robinson / L.P. Young (Vincent Special)
3rd W.G. Boddice / W. Canning (Norton)
Fastest lap: R. Robinson (Vincent Special) 78.66mph (new record)

Bernard qualified for the final of the 350cc event by finishing second in his heat and finished a respectable third in the final behind R. Anderson and G.B. Tanner on Nortons.

350cc Solo Final (10 laps)
1st R. Anderson (Norton) 79.55mph
2nd G.B. Tanner (Norton)
3rd B.D. Codd (Norton)
4th G.C.A. Murphy (AJS)
5th D. Minter (Norton)
6th E. Minihan (Norton)
Fastest lap: R. Anderson (Norton) 81.97mph

1000cc Non-Experts Race (6 laps)
1st B.L. Denehy (Norton) 74.75mph
2nd J.F. Stracey (Spud / Triumph)
3rd L.A. James (Vincent Comet)
Fastest lap: J.F. Stracey (Spud / Vincent) 78.83mph

Sidecar Handicap Race (8 laps)
1st J.C.T. Parker / H.G. Collins (499cc BSA) 65.01mph
2nd T. Folwell / P. Knocker (Matchless)
3rd R.J. Ireland / D. Wallen (Norton)
Fastest lap: C. Smith / E. Bliss (Norton) 78.47mph

R. Anderson (Norton) won the Senior 500cc race, leading from start to finish and slowly pulling further away on each lap. Geoff Tanner (Norton) fought his way from fourth place to finish second and in doing so posted the fastest lap of the race at 83mph. D. Minter (Norton), J.R. Clarke (Moto Guzzi) and G.C.A. Murphy (Matchless) had a race-long battle for third place with Minter coming out the winner. Bernard was listed in the programme as one of the reserves in this event and it is not known if he even got a chance to start the race.

500cc Senior Solo Race (12 laps)
1st R. Anderson (Norton) 81.05mph
2nd G.B. Tanner (Norton)
3rd D. Minter (Norton)
4th G.C.A. Murphy (Matchless)
5th J.R. Clarke (Moto Guzzi)
6th F.A. Rutherford (Duke-BSA)

The Louth Standard reported on Friday 10th May that on Monday 6th Bernard had taken delivery of a new 500cc Norton.

Mallory Park on 12th May 1957 was the wettest meeting in the short history of the circuit to date. The riders treated the track surface with a lot of respect because of the wet conditions and, as a result of this, there were very few accidents.

As well as the usual programme of races this was the meeting organised by The Leicester Query Club that counted as one of four rounds in the East Midland Centre A.C.U. Club Team Championship. There was a total of ten clubs in the competition, each consisting of a team of three riders. The clubs involved were Banovallum, Bolsover, Derby Phoenix, Ilkeston, Leicester Query, Loughborough & District, Mansfield, Nottingham Tornado, Pathfinders and Lincoln. The four rounds contested were this Road Racing event at Mallory, a Flat Grass event held at Boston, a Trial event organised by the East Midland Centre Club and a Scramble meeting organised by the Banovallum Club. For the Mallory meeting Bernard was riding for the Mansfield Club alongside George Catlin and B. Freestone (in the programme it looks as though Freestone was replaced by H. Crowder). Points were awarded in each heat (12 points for first place down to 1 point for 12th place) and the total at the end of the six heats that were contested on the day determined the winning team. The results of the six heats were:

Heat One

1st J. Eckart (Leicester Query) 4m 20.8sec, (12 points)
2nd R. Jervis (Nottingham Tornado) 4m 25.4sec, (11 points)
3rd G. Catlin (Mansfield) 4m 33sec, (10 points)

Heat Two

1st F. Wallis (Nottingham Tornado) 4m 31.6sec, (12 points)
2nd N.H. Storer (Pathfinders) 4m 33.8sec, (11 points)
3rd P.H. Tait (Leicester Query) 5m 44.8sec, (10 points)

Heat Three

1st B.D. Codd (Mansfield) 4m 44.4sec, (12 points)
2nd A.G. Briggs (Pathfinders) 5m 2.8sec, (11 points)
3rd A. Evans (Leicester Query) 5m 3.4sec (10 points)

Heat Four

1st F. Wallis (Nottingham Tornado) 4m 44.8sec, (12 points)
2nd A.G. Briggs (Pathfinders) 4m 47.8sec, (11 points)
3rd G. Catlin (Mansfield) 4m 53.8sec, (10 points)

Heat Five

1st P.H. Tait (Leicester Query) 4m 53.4sec, (12 points)
2nd B. Lawrence (Nottingham Tornado) 4m 57.6sec, (11 points)
3rd P. Minion (Pathfinders) 5m 6.8sec, (10 points)

Heat Six

1st B.D. Codd (Mansfield) 4m 33.8sec, (12 points)
2nd N.H. Storer (Pathfinders) 4m 34.4sec, (11 points)
3rd R. Jervis (Nottingham Tornado) 4m 48.4sec, (10 points)

Despite good results in their respective heats from Bernard and George Catlin representing the Mansfield Club they could only finish fourth with the Nottingham Tornado Club winning by 3 points. The Nottingham Tornado Team consisted of R. Jervis, F. Wallis and D. Nourish. Second equal were the Pathfinders Team of A.G. Briggs, P. Minion and N.H. Storer and the Leicester Query Club represented by J. Eckart, P.H. Tait and A. Evans.

1st Nottingham Tornado, 65 points
2nd = Pathfinders & Leicester Query, 62 points
4th Mansfield, 57 points
5th Ilkeston, 49 points
6th Lincoln, 35 points
7th Bolsover, 29 points
8th = Banovallum and Loughborough & District 27 points
10th Derby Phoenix, 18 points

There were two heats in the 250cc event with the first ten in each heat qualifying for the final:

250cc Solo Heats (5 laps)
Heat One

1st R.W. Good (250cc Excelsior) 6m 17.4sec, 64.42mph
2nd P. Tomes (248cc JAP) 6m 19.4sec
3rd J. Murgatroyd (248cc Velocette) 6m 19.6sec

250cc Solo Heat Two

1st T.E. Fenwick (248cc Moto Guzzi) 6m 15.4sec, 64.73mph
2nd H.R. Hutchinson (250cc Triumph) 6m 15.6sec
3rd A.G. Briggs (248cc Lomas Enfield) 6m 17sec

250cc Solo Final (8 laps)

1st J. Murgatroyd (248cc Velocette) 8m 24sec, 67.5mph
2nd A.G. Briggs (248cc Lomas Enfield) 8m 34.6sec
3rd R.W. Good (250cc Excelsior) 8m 55.6sec

Sidecar Final for machines up to 1000cc (8 laps)
1st C. Smith (500cc Norton) 8m 3.6sec, 70.35mph
2nd F. Taylor (499cc Norton)
3rd C. Freeman (499cc Norton)

Sidecar Handicap Final (10 laps)
1st P.E.W. Russell (499cc Norton) 12m 21.8sec, 65.1mph
2nd F. Hanks (499cc Norton)
3rd C. Smith (500cc Norton)

Bernard was in the second heat of three for the 251cc to 350cc event and won it by just over 15 seconds. The first seven in each heat qualified for the Final. The heat results were:

350cc Solo Heats (5 laps)
Heat One
1st B. Purslow (Velocette) 5m 41.6sec
2nd K.H. Patrick (350cc BSA) 5m 42.8sec
3rd P. Ferbrache (349cc Norton)

350cc Solo Heat Two
1st B.D. Codd (350cc Norton) 5m 59.8sec, 67.91mph
2nd P.D. Chatterton (348cc Norton) 6m 15sec
3rd G. Downes (350cc AJS) 6m 16sec

350cc Solo Heat Three
1st R.W. Good (350cc Norton) 5m 59.9sec, 67.54mph
2nd J. Eckart (348cc BSA) 6m 8.8sec,
3rd M.T. Brookes (349cc Norton) 6m 12.4sec

350cc Solo Final (8 laps)
1st B. Purslow (348cc Velocette) 8m 3.4sec, 70.38mph
2nd K.H. Patrick (350cc BSA) 8m 6.4sec
3rd F. Wallis (348cc BSA)
4th B.D. Codd (350cc Norton)

Bernard was the holder of the 350cc lap record for both 5 laps (5m 20.8sec, 75.75mph) and 8 laps (8m 19.4sec, 77.85mph).

There were also three heats in the 340cc up to 1000cc Solo class and the results were:

1000cc Solo Heats (5 laps)
Heat One
1st F. Wallis (499cc BSA) 5m 48.4sec, 69.74mph
2nd P. Middleton (499cc Norton) 5m 49.2sec
3rd M.T. Brookes (498cc Triumph) 5m 52.8sec
4th B.D. Codd (500cc Norton)

Heat Two
1st R.W. Good (350cc Norton) 6m 0.8sec, 67.35mph
2nd R. Fay (500cc Norton) 6m 1.8sec
3rd A.G. Briggs (349cc JAP/Triumph) 6m 6sec

Heat Three
1st N.H. Storer (499cc Norton) 5m 41.6sec, 71.13mph
2nd B. Purslow (499cc Norton) 5m 42sec
3rd P. Ferbrache (499cc Norton) 5m 42.4sec

1000cc Solo Final (8 laps)
1st R. Fay (500cc Norton) 7m 38.8sec, 74.15mph
2nd B. Purslow (499cc Norton) 7m 40.8sec
3rd N.H. Storer (499cc Norton) 7m 41.6sec
4th B.D. Codd (500cc Norton) 7m 44.4sec

Bernard was again involved in the 251cc up to 500cc event, and there were three heats with the first seven in each heat qualifying for the final.

500cc Solo Heats (5 laps)
Heat One
1st N.H. Storer (499cc Norton) 5m 34.4sec, 72.66mph
2nd T.E. Fenwick (Moto Guzzi) 5m 50sec
3rd A.H. Frost (499cc Norton) 5m 54sec

Heat Two
1st R. Fay (500cc Norton) 5m 34.8sec, 72.62mph
2nd B. Purslow (499cc Norton) 5m 35.8sec
3rd F. Wallis (499cc BSA) 5m 40.8sec

Heat Three
1st B.D. Codd (500cc Norton) 5m 43sec
2nd G. Lowe (499cc BSA) 6m 1sec
3rd P.H. Tait (500cc Norton)

500cc Solo Final (8 laps)
1st R. Fay (500cc Norton) 7m 35sec, 76.41mph
2nd P. Middleton (499cc Norton)
3rd B. Purslow (499cc Norton)
4th B.D. Codd (500cc Norton)

Bernard travelled over to Northern Ireland next for the International North West "200" Road Race, which was run on 18th May 1957 and raced on the street circuit known as "The Triangle" between the towns of Portstewart, Coleraine and Portrush in the Causeway Coast and Glens. The event was established in 1929 and was originally a 200-mile race run on a 11.1-mile-circuit and was renowned as being one of the fastest circuits in the world of motorcycle racing. The first race was run on 20th April 1929 and included some legendary names such as Stanley Woods, Percy "Tim" Hunt, and Ernie Nott. The race was eventually won though by W.J. McCracken on a 348cc Velocette in a time of 3h 8m 35sec, with his fastest lap at over 67mph. It is still considered one of the most exciting races on the motor sport calendar, with modern day superbikes reaching speeds in excess of 200mph and average speeds of 120mph. The outright lap record is held by Tom Herron with a speed of 127.63mph, set in 1978. Since then, as machines have become a lot faster, the course has been modified with the introduction of chicanes to make it slower in places and safer. The current lap record is held by Lincolnshire rider Steve Plater with a speed of 124.109mph posted in 2006.

In 2004 Michael Rutter was the first rider to record a top speed in excess of 200mph and in 2012 Martin Jessop set a new fastest speed trap time of 208mph in a practice session. Before the event in 1957 the average lap speed was still under 100mph. There had been improvements made to the track surface since the previous year, including eliminating a challenging bend and potential bottleneck, replacing it with a faster, smoother banked section which resulted in the organisers expecting quicker lap times. This effectively shortened the course by 35 yards as well, so comparing lap speeds and times over the years is really quite irrelevant.

Even though the race clashed with the German Grand Prix at Hockenheim there was a strong list of entrants, including Alastair King, Bob Anderson, Jack Brett, and John Hartle as well as Bernard who was to compete in the 350cc class.

Jack Brett (Norton) got a good start in the 500cc race leading the 25 starters into the first part of the lap, but it was Geoff Tanner (Norton) who was leading after the first lap with a standing start lap of 94.6mph. Tanner increased his lead to 12 seconds by the third lap with Ken Patrick (Norton) in third place. Fourth was Wilf Herron, also on a Norton. Brett took the lead on the eighth lap when Tanner came into the pits to refuel. When he rejoined the race, in trying to make some of the lost time up he increased the lap record to 99.79mph. Jack Brett on his 499cc Norton made history on the eleventh lap by posting a lap of 6m 37sec which equated to a speed of 100.03mph. Geoff Tanner retired soon after this, leaving Brett to win easily by over seven minutes. K.H. Patrick (Norton) was second and Jack Wood was third. The weather deteriorated and rain fell on sections of the course (which reduced the lap times) so Brett's record was not threatened.

The 350cc race was started just one minute after the 500cc start, with Bob Anderson (Norton) getting a good start. His first lap was 90.95mph, which was impressive from a standing start. Arthur Wheeler (Moto Guzzi) was already 24 seconds behind in second place with Bob Brown on Geoff Dukes' streamlined Velocette third. Anderson was soon lapping at an average of 93.95mph which meant he was soon involved with the slower 500cc machines. He improved his lap times to 95.73mph and eventually his best lap was 95.96mph, winning by over four minutes. Considering the quality of the 34 riders that started the 350cc race Bernard finished a very creditable fifth.

Sammy Miller (NSU) won the 250cc event even though he was last-but-one off the start line when his NSU was reluctant to fire up but, once it did, he made short work of getting to the front of the pack with an average lap speed of 88.09mph. By half-race distance Miller had lapped every other rider in the 250cc class. Second place went to F. Purslow (NSU), and H. Kirby (Velocette) was third.

500cc Race (18 laps)

1st J. Brett (499cc Norton) 2h 2m 58sec, 96.88mph

2nd K.H. Patrick (Norton) 2h 10m 14sec,91.48mph

3rd J.J. Wood (Norton)
4th W. Herron (Norton)
5th G.T. Salt (Norton)
6th F. Yeates (Norton)
Fastest lap: J. Brett (499cc Norton) 6m 37sec, 10003mph (New lap Record)

350cc Race (17 laps)
1st R. Anderson (Norton) 2h 1m 49sec, 93.13mph
2nd W.A. Holmes (Norton) 2h 6m 27sec, 88.98mph
3rd J. Buchan (Norton) 2h 8m 13sec, 87.76mph
4th A.F. Wheeler (Moto Guzzi)
5th B.D. Codd (Norton)
6th B.F. Purslow (Norton)
Fastest lap: R. Anderson (Norton) 6m 55sec, 95.96mph (New lap Record)

250cc Race (16 laps)
1st S.H. Miller (NSU) 2h 1m 18sec, 87.30mph
2nd F. Purslow (NSU)
3rd H. Kirby (Velocette)
4th F. Telfer (Norton)
5th W.G. Dehany (Velocette)
Fastest lap: S.H. Miller (NSU) 7m 24sec, 89.44mph

Open Handicap
1st R. Anderson (Norton)
2nd W.A. Holmes (Norton)
3rd H. Kirby (Velocette)

500cc Handicap
1st K.H. Patrick (Norton)
2nd A.E. Sutherland (BSA)
3rd W. Herron (Norton)

350cc Handicap
1st W.A. Holmes (Norton)
2nd J. Buchan (Norton)
3rd M.T. Brookes (Norton)

250cc Handicap
1st H. Kirby (Velocette)
2nd W.G. Dehany (Velocette)
3rd I.F. Telfer (Norton)

First time competitor Handicap
1st K.H. Patrick (Norton)
2nd G.T. Salt (Norton)
3rd M.T. Brookes (Norton)

Club Team Award:
Bay of Plenty (New Zealand) H.B. Lowe, I.F. Yeates and F.R. Cameron.

CHAPTER NINE

THE GOLDEN JUBILEE TT RACES

"He will do well to finish somewhere between ninth and twelfth"

Bernard's ambition to win the International TT was now to be a possibility as he was entered in the Golden Jubilee Races of 1957 by his sponsor, Hallens of Cambridge Ltd riding the 348cc Norton in the Junior event and the relatively new 499cc Norton in the Senior race.

There were 89 entries for the Junior event and 88 for the Senior. This was one of the biggest and most prestigious events of the year and attracted attention from the Italian works Factory Teams such as MV Agusta, Moto Guzzi and Gilera. Geoff Duke was initially down to ride the Factory Gilera but because he was still recovering from a shoulder injury he had sustained racing at Imola in a World Championship event his place was taken by the Australian rider Bob Brown, who would be team-mate to Bob McIntyre. It was thought that Britain's best hopes of a victory were in the hands of John Hartle, Jack Brett and Alan Trow who were all riding Nortons. R.H. "Dickie" Dale riding the Moto Guzzi was also an early favourite for the Junior race win.

Saturday 25th May was the first practice session. The best lap times for the Seniors were:

1st J. Hartle (Norton) 24m 12sec, 93.58mph
2nd G.A. Murphy (Matchless) 24m 28.6sec, 92.48mph
3rd W. Zeller (BMW) 25m 14.8sec, 89.67mph
4th J.J. Wood (Norton) 25m 17.4sec, 89.51mph
5th K. Bryen (Matchless) 25m 35sec, 88.49mph
6th A.J. Trow (Norton) 25m 51sec, 87.57mph

The best practice lap times for the Junior event were:

1st J. Brett (Norton) 25m 23.4sec, 89.16mph
2nd G.A. Murphy (AJS) 25m 49.4sec, 87.66mph
3rd D. Christian (AJS) 25m 50.6sec, 87.59mph
4th A. King (Norton) 25m 55sec, 87.35mph

5th G.R. Costain (Norton) 26m 06.2sec, 86.73mph
6th J.B. Denton (BSA) 26m 30.8sec, 85.38mph

It was greatly anticipated that this would be the year that the first 100mph lap would be posted in the Senior TT event but after the first practice session it was clear to see there was a lot of work to do to make that possible. Monday's lap times did improve greatly, with Bob McIntyre setting a fast pace on the Gilera and lapping 57 seconds quicker than John Hartle had done in the first session on his Norton. The weather and track conditions were near-perfect for the 4.45am start of practice, unlike the afternoon session when the warm sun had melted the tarmac track surface at numerous parts of the circuit, particularly at Quarry Bends and Laurel Bank. Three riders had incidents due to the melting tar: J. Buchan (Norton) and Walter Zeller (BMW) both crashed at Laurel Bank and Derick Minter came off his Norton going into Ramsey. The sun also posed a problem for the riders later in the evening when they complained of poor visibility as it was setting. Bernard finished the session sixth fastest on his 499cc Norton, which was an impressive performance considering the quality of the competition. One newspaper reporter had commented on Bernard saying, *"He will do well to finish somewhere between ninth and twelfth."* The best lap times on Monday May 27th for the Seniors in the morning session were:

1st R. McIntyre (Gilera) 23m 15sec, 97.37mph
2nd T.S. Shepherd (MV Agusta) 23m 45.4sec, 95.29mph
3rd J. Surtees (MV Agusta) 24m 03sec, 94.13mph
4th R.H. Dale (Moto Guzzi) 24m 55.2sec, 90.84mph
5th D.G. Chapman (Norton) 25m 15.2sec, 89.65mph
6th B.D. Codd (Norton) 25m 21.4sec, 89.26mph

The Junior lap times for the morning session were:

1st R. McIntyre (Gilera) 24m 02.6sec, 94.15mph
2nd R.H. Dale (Moto Guzzi) 24m 15.6sec, 93.31mph
3rd J. Hartle (Norton) 24m 31sec, 92.34mph
4th K.R. Campbell (Moto Guzzi) 24m 44.4sec, 91.50mph
5th A. King (Norton) 25m 04.2sec, 90.30mph
6th G.A. Murphy (AJS) 25m 07.8sec, 90.08mph

Afternoon practice saw Bernard, Dickie Dale, and Bob McIntyre out on their Junior machines after posting respectable times in the morning on their Senior bikes. Bob McIntyre was fastest with Bernard again finishing sixth. P.A. Davey (BSA) was one of the riders who recorded a speed of over 100mph on the Sulby Mile in the evening practice session, his actual speed being 112.50mph. Best lap times in the afternoon for the Seniors were:

1st J. Surtees (MV Agusta) 23m 31.6sec, 96.22mph
2nd J. Brett (Norton) 23m 47.4sec, 95.15mph
3rd T.S. Shepherd (MV Agusta) 24m 09.2sec, 93.73mph
4th R. Anderson (Norton) 24m 17.6sec, 93.18mph
5th A.J. Trow (Norton) 24m 30sec, 92.40mph
6th J.J. Wood (Norton) 24m 48.4sec, 91.27mph

Best Junior lap times were:

1st R. McIntyre (Gilera) 23m 37sec, 95.86mph
2nd J. Hartle (Norton) 24m 11sec, 93.61mph
3rd R.H. Dale (Moto Guzzi) 24m 27.4sec, 92.56mph
4th E. Hinton (Norton) 25m 13sec, 89.77mph
5th A. King (Norton) 25m 27.8sec, 88.90mph
6th B.D. Codd (Norton) 26m 16.4sec, 86.17mph

Melting tar was still an issue during the morning of Tuesday 28th for practice but it did not deter Bob McIntyre from posting a quick lap from a standing start on his four-cylinder Gilera and then producing a stunning time of 22m 47.8sec, which equated to a speed of 99.3mph on his Teammate (Bob Brown's) machine. Second and third fastest were J. Surtees and T.S. Shepherd who were sharing the use of an MV Agusta until more machines could be delivered from the factory in Italy. To show how important this meeting was to the factory teams, when the MV Agustas did arrive there were 18 machines of various capacities while the Moto Guzzi factory had already sent nine machines including two Senior V-8s transported in four lorries from Italy, with more on the way.

To think just 21 months earlier Bernard had taken his BSA Goldstar to his first Road Race meeting at Snetterton in a pig trailer and now he was competing with and at times beating some of the best motorcycle racers in the world. Tuesday afternoon lap times for the Senior event were:

1st R. McIntyre (Gilera) 22m 47.8sec, 99.30mph
2nd J. Surtees (MV Agusta) 23m 10sec, 97.72mph
3rd T.S. Shepherd (MV Agusta) 23m 24.4sec, 96.71mph
4th R. Fay (Norton) 23m 40.6sec, 95.61mph
5th J. Hartle (Norton) 23m 47.4sec, 95.15mph
6th K.R. Campbell (Moto Guzzi) 24m 33.4sec, 92.18mph

Best Junior times were:

1st R.H. Dale (Moto Guzzi) 24m 43.8sec, 91.54mph
2nd A.J. Trow (Norton) 25m 08.4sec, 90.05mph
3rd D.V. Chadwick (Velocette) 25m 15.8sec, 89.61mph
4th J.D. Anderson (AJS) 26m 06.2sec, 86.73mph
5th P.H. Tait (Norton) 26m 20.2sec, 85.96mph
6th F.M. Fox (Norton) 26m 23.6sec, 85.77mph

Practice sessions continued on Wednesday 29th, Thursday 30th and Friday 31st but no record of Bernard can be found, although it is known that he didn't finish in the top six places any more in either the Junior or Senior practice sessions, so his best time in each class was 25m 21.4sec, 89.26mph on the 500cc machine, and 26m 16.4sec, 86.17mph on the 350cc Norton. Bob McIntyre dominated the remaining practice sessions in the Senior class finishing second on the Wednesday with a time of 23m 22.8sec, a speed of 96.82mph behind W. Zeller (BMW) who posted a time of 23m 21.6sec, 96.91mph. McIntyre was fastest on Thursday and Friday with times of 23m 23.4sec, 96.78mph and 23m 05.4sec, 98.04mph respectively. Still the 100mph lap of the mountain course was proving elusive.

In the Junior class J. Brett (Norton) was quickest on Wednesday with a time of 23m 56.0sec, 94.59mph, and R.H. Dale (Moto Guzzi) was fastest on Thursday with a time of 23m 55.4sec, 94.62mph. (In posting this fastest lap Dale beat the previous lap record of 23m 56sec, 94.61mph, which was held by the late Ray Amm who set his time during the 1954 race). Brian Freestone crashed his Norton in Thursday's Junior practice session and had to be taken to Noble's Hospital with multiple injuries. He had previously posted a time of 25m 32sec on his Senior Norton machine. R. McIntyre was quickest on Friday with a time of 23m 56.0sec, 94.61mph.

Race day for the Junior TT of 1957 was Monday 3rd June. Despite a misty start to the day, conditions were perfect at 11.00 am for the start of the Junior race. G.T. Salt (BSA) was the first rider away from the start line. J. Brett (Norton) was the first rider to cross the line after the first lap but was only in fifth place on corrected time even though he had made up eight places. His time was 24m 30.8sec, 92.35mph. It was R. McIntyre who led at the end of lap one with a stunning time of 23m 14.2sec a speed of 97.42mph. This meant that the lap record had been reduced by 41.8 seconds from a standing start. It was only 35.2 seconds slower than Geoff Duke's Senior lap record of 22m 39sec at a speed of 99.97mph. "Dickie" Dale (Moto Guzzi) had the advantage of a larger than usual fuel tank which meant he could complete the race without a fuel stop compared to Bob McIntyre on the Gilera who would have to make a pit stop after three laps. Dale's first lap was 23m 58.8sec. The Leader board after lap one was:

1st R. McIntyre (Gilera) 23m 14.2sec, 97.42mph
2nd R.H. Dale (Moto Guzzi) 23m 58.8sec, 94.40mph
3rd J. Hartle (Norton) 24m 05.4sec, 93.97mph
4th J. Surtees (MV Agusta) 24m 16.8sec, 93.23mph
5th J. Brett (Norton) 24m 30.8sec, 92.35mph
6th K.R. Campbell (Moto Guzzi) 24m 34sec, 92.15mph

Bernard completed his first lap in a time of 25m 35sec, but I don't know what position that would place him in.

The first eight riders were all lapping at over 90mph, and five different makes of machine were in the first five places.

McIntyre had to make an unscheduled pit stop to replace his sparkplug after the first lap, which put Dale into the lead with J. Hartle on the single cylinder Norton in second place and McIntyre pushed back to third. The leader board after lap two was:

1st R.H. Dale (Moto Guzzi) 47m 31.8sec, 95.28mph
2nd J. Hartle (Norton) 48m 00sec, 94.33mph
3rd R. McIntyre (Gilera) 48m 02sec, 94.27mph
4th J. Brett (Norton) 48m 34.4sec, 93.23mph
5th K.R. Campbell (Moto Guzzi) 48m 48.4sec, 92.77mph
6th R.N. Brown (Gilera) 49m 08.4sec, 92.15mph

Bernard's second lap was 25m 22.8sec

At the end of the third lap Dale was still leading from Hartle in second and McIntyre, despite riding well and making up time, was back in third place with Jack Brett still in fourth place. John Surtees on the MV Agusta had moved up from tenth to seventh place. The leader board after lap three showed:

1st R.H. Dale (Moto Guzzi) 1h 11m 20sec, 95.22mph
2nd J. Hartle (Norton) 1h 11m 51sec, 94.53mph
3rd R. McIntyre (Gilera) 1h 12m 16.2sec, 93.99mph
4th J. Brett (Norton) 1h 12m 57sec, 93.11mph
5th K.R. Campbell (Moto Guzzi) 1h 13m 02sec, 93.00mph
6th R.N. Brown (Gilera) 1h 13m 18.6sec, 92.66mph

Bernard's third lap was 26m 33.8sec

Dale was able to stay in front of J. Hartle (Norton) in second place and R. McIntyre in third until he had to pit on the third lap when a bird hit his fairing and broke his screen. This cost him over three and a half minutes having a new screen fitted and he lost all chance of winning the race after that.

McIntyre's pits stop at the beginning of lap four to take on fuel and oil took 40 seconds, compared to Jack Brett's stop taking just 20 seconds. The average race speed after three laps was a staggering 95.22mph. There were a lot of retirements on the fourth lap, with J. Brett stopping after the Guthrie Memorial with engine trouble, and at Quarry Bends the oil tank on J.J. Wood's Norton burst, spilling oil on the track. J. Hartle hit the oil patch and lost control of his machine and crashed resulting in him requiring medical attention. "Dickie" Dale also crashed on the oil and had to retire because his Moto Guzzi was too badly damaged to continue. This put McIntyre back in the lead, completing the fourth lap with an average speed of 93.72mph. Keith Campbell (Moto Guzzi) was second and McIntyre's teammate R.N. Brown third. John Surtees moved up to fourth place but was 90 seconds behind Brown. The leader board after lap four showed:

1st R. McIntyre (Gilera) 1h 36m 38sec, 93.72mph
2nd K.R. Campbell (Moto Guzzi) 1h 37m 16.4sec, 93.10mph
3rd R.N. Brown (Gilera) 1h 37m 27sec, 92.93mph
4th J. Surtees (MV Agusta) 1h 39m 02.4sec,91.16mph

5th G.A. Murphy (AJS) 1h 40m 35sec, 90.04mph
6th E. Hinton (Norton) 1h 40m 36.8sec, 90.01mph

Bernard's fourth lap was 28m 30.6sec

There was no change on the leader board on lap five, but John Surtees (MV Agusta) did make some ground up on R.N. Brown's Gilera. There were also a lot of retirements on lap five. The leader board was:

1st R. McIntyre (Gilera) 1h 59m 55.2sec, 94.40mph
2nd K.R. Campbell (Moto Guzzi) 2h 01m 34.6sec, 93.11mph
3rd R.N. Brown (Gilera) 2h 02m 40sec, 92.38mph
4th J. Surtees (MV Agusta) 2h 03m 38.4sec, 91.56mph
5th E. Hinton (Norton) 2h 05m 18.6sec, 90.34mph
6th G.A. Murphy (AJS) 2h 05m 27sec, 90.24mph

Bernard's fifth lap was 26m 10.8sec

There was now no one left to challenge McIntyre, and he was pulling out a substantial lead over Campbell. The second four-cylinder Gilera of Brown was over a minute behind in third place with J. Surtees in fourth. Bernard had been reported as going well up to this point. The leader board was much the same as the previous lap:

1st R. McIntyre (Gilera) 2h 23m 13.4sec, 94.85mph
2nd K.R. Campbell (Moto Guzzi) 2h 25m 55.6sec, 93.08mph
3rd R.N. Brown (Gilera) 2h 27m 04.6sec, 92.36mph
4th J. Surtees (MV Agusta) 2h 28m 07.6sec, 91.70mph
5th E. Hinton (Norton) 2h 30m 03sec, 90.53mph
6th G.A. Murphy (AJS) 2h 30m 17sec, 90.39mph

Bernard's sixth lap was 27m 06sec

As Bernard crossed the line to start his last lap, he indicated to his pit crew that something was wrong by giving them the thumbs down signal. He was forced to retire later in the lap. The final lap was uneventful for McIntyre, and he took the chequered flag by a substantial margin even though he had slowed on his last two laps. His last lap time was 23m 36.8sec, which was 20 seconds slower than the previous two laps and 22.6 seconds slower than his record lap. The

Senior TT result was:

1st R. McIntyre (Gilera) 2h 46m 50.2sec, 94.99mph
2nd K.R. Campbell (Moto Guzzi) 2h 50m 29.8sec, 92.95mph
3rd R.N. Brown (Gilera) 2h 51m 38.2sec, 92.34mph
4th J. Surtees (MV Agusta) 2h 52m 37.6sec, 91.80mph
5th E. Hinton (Norton) 2h 54m 50sec, 90.65mph
6th G.A. Murphy (AJS) 2h 55m 08.4sec, 90.49mph
Fastest Lap: R. McIntyre (Gilera) 23m 14.2sec 97.42mph (new record)

Of the 78 starters, 53 completed the race

In the winner's enclosure Bob McIntyre told reporters that he had to complete the second lap with his Gilera running on only three of its four cylinders because of an oiled-up spark plug. Second place finisher Keith Campbell told reporters that he nearly crashed his Moto Guzzi at Ramsey Hairpin and only just saw the patch of oil in time at Quarry Bends that had caught out "Dickie" Dale and John Hartle.

On close inspection of the first three machines home, they all looked to be in perfect condition considering what they had been put through. Tyres were worn, although not too badly; chain tension and clutch and brake controls were good, as was engine wear. The manufacturer's Team Award could not be presented as no Team finished the race intact. The Club Team Award went to B.M.C.R.C. which consisted of R. McIntyre (Gilera), J. Surtees (MV Agusta) and A.F. Wheeler (Moto Guzzi). Silver Replicas were awarded to the first 26 finishers and bronze Replicas awarded to the 27th to 49th place finishers.

Bernard's fastest lap of the race was his second lap with a time of 25m 22.8sec. The highest placed Lincolnshire rider was George Catlin (Norton) who finished 22nd and had an average speed of 85.26mph, therefore being one of the riders to receive a silver Replica. B.H. Lilley (Norton) of Holbeach finished 41st and received a bronze Replica of the famous TT Trophy. Peter Davey (BSA) of Sleaford was forced to retire with engine trouble after going well for four laps.

The Senior TT race was held on Friday 7th June. The race was due to start at 11.00am but proceedings commenced at 10.00am when the enclosure gates were opened for a procession, which included past TT winners and a collection of vintage machines that made their way from Craig-ny-Baa along the course to the grandstand. The weather was perfect, as were the road conditions all round the course. Everyone was anticipating the first 100mph lap of the mountain course; the only question was who would be the man to achieve it. With the absence of Geoff Duke and Bill Lomas, who were both unable to participate due to injury, the favourites were undoubtably Dickie Dale on the V-8 Moto Guzzi, Bob McIntyre on the four-cylinder Gilera or maybe last year's winner John Surtees on the MV Agusta. It would almost certainly be an Italian machine and more than likely a British rider. John Hartle was still recovering from his accident in the Junior race (when he crashed on the oil patch) and didn't start but Dickie Dale, although he was still suffering from bruising, was on the grid.

This was the first year that the Senior event was to be an eight-lap race and all the riders except for the three Moto Guzzi 500cc single-cylinder machines were going to have to make a stop to re-fuel. Jack Brett was the first rider to push-start his Norton and negotiate Bray Hill with the other competitors starting at ten-second intervals behind him. He understood he had to make a good start and take advantage of the clear roads ahead of him if he was to be able to compete with the faster multi-cylinder bikes that would be pursuing him for the next 301.86 miles.

Brett's first lap was nothing exceptional: he recorded a time of 23m 58.6sec, 94.41mph which was only good enough to put him in sixth place after the first lap. Dickie Dale's time of 23m 53.4sec was not as quick as expected either so it was beginning to look as though conditions were not as perfect as first thought, until Bob McIntyre completed his first lap with a time of 22m 38.4sec, a speed of 99.99mph which beat Geoff Dukes' existing lap record by 0.6 seconds and this from a standing start. Surely the much talked-about 100mph lap was going to be a reality at last. The leader board at the end of lap one was:

1st R. McIntyre (Gilera) 22m 38.4sec, 99.99mph
2nd J. Surtees (MV Agusta) 23m 17.4sec,97.20mph
3rd W. Zeller (BMW) 23m 44.2sec, 95.35mph
4th R.H. Dale (Moto Guzzi) 23m 53.4sec, 94.76mph
5th R.N. Brown (Gilera) 23m 56.8sec, 94.53mph
6th J. Brett (Norton) 23m 58.6sec, 94.41mph

Bernard's first lap time was 24m 53.8sec

On the second lap, McIntyre kept up the blistering pace and increased his lead on J. Surtees to 30 seconds. By the time he reached Ramsey he was one minute ahead. McIntyre completed his second lap with a time of 22m 24.4sec and 101.03mph; his average for the first two laps was 100.52mph and so finally the milestone had been achieved. Surtees was in a secure second place with a time of 23m 3.6sec. The leader board after lap two was:

1st R. McIntyre (Gilera) 45m 02.8sec, 100.52mph
2nd J. Surtees (MV Agusta) 46m 21sec, 97.70mph
3rd W. Zeller (BMW) 47m 07.2sec, 96.10mph
4th R.H. Dale (Moto Guzzi) 47m 17sec, 95.77mph
5th R.N. Brown (Gilera) 47m 27.4sec, 95.45mph
6th J. Brett (Norton) 47m 32.2sec, 95.26mph

Bernard's lap time on the second lap was 24m 49.2sec

McIntyre was catching Surtees on the road and on lap three he was 21.8 seconds quicker than the MV Agusta rider even though he posted a slower lap time than on previous laps. McIntyre's speed was 100.54mph compared to Surtees at 98.86mph the leader board at the end of lap three was:

1st R. McIntyre (Gilera) 1h 07m 33.8sec, 100.53mph
2nd J. Surtees (MV Agusta) 1h 09m 13.8sec, 98.11mph
3rd W. Zeller (BMW) 1h 10m 14.2sec, 96.71mph
4th R.H. Dale (Moto Guzzi) 1h 10m 29.2sec, 96.37mph
5th R.N. Brown (Gilera) 1h 10m 48sec, 95.94mph
6th J. Brett (Norton) 1h 10m 57.6sec, 95.72mph

Bernard's third lap was 25m 31.2sec

McIntyre increased his lead even more on the fourth lap, posting a time of 22m 23.2sec and pushing the lap record to 101.12mph. He now led Surtees by 2m 10.2sec and was just 9.8 seconds behind him on the road. Walter Zeller had ignition problems with his BMW and retired at Ramsey. Dale also stopped at Sulby but restarted and completed the lap but, when he came into re-fuel, his Moto Guzzi was certainly not running as well as it had been and, as a result, he lost fourth place. The leader board after lap four was:

1st R. McIntyre (Gilera) 1h 29m 57sec, 100.68mph
2nd J. Surtees (MV Agusta) 1h 32m 07.2sec, 98.31mph

3rd R.N. Brown (Gilera) 1h 33m 59sec, 96.36mph
4th J. Brett (Norton) 1h 34m 19.6sec, 96.01mph
5th R.H. Dale (Moto Guzzi) 1h 34m 45.2sec, 95.58mph
6th G.B. Tanner (Norton) 1h 35m 43.4sec, 94.61mph

Bernard's time for lap four was 25m 13.4sec

On lap five the inevitable happened and McIntyre took the lead on the road by passing Surtees and by the end of the lap he had increased the lead to 25 yards. The positions at the end of lap five were:

1st R. McIntyre (Gilera) 1h 53m 35.4sec, 99.66mph
2nd J. Surtees (MV Agusta) 1h 55m 55.6sec, 97.65mph
3rd R.N. Brown (Gilera) 1h 57m 58.4sec, 95.96mph
4th J. Brett (Norton) 1h 58m 28sec, 95.56mph
5th K.R. Campbell (Moto Guzzi) 1h 59m 45.8sec, 94.52mph
6th R.H. Dale (Moto Guzzi) 1h 59m 56.6sec, 94.38mph

Bernard's time for lap five was 24m 34.8sec

McIntyre continued to increase his lead on the sixth lap and by the end of the lap he was 23.6 seconds clear of Surtees on the road. The result of this was another stunning lap time of 22m 33.6sec which equated to a speed of 100.35mph. Unless something catastrophic happened it was McIntyre who was going to take the win. At this point his average race speed was 99.7mph - was it possible he could complete the eight laps with an average speed of over 100mph?

In stopping to re-fuel, Geoff Tanner had lost his sixth-place position to Dickie Dale and Campbell had moved up to fifth place on the other Moto Guzzi. The leader board after lap six was:

1st R. McIntyre (Gilera) 2h 16m 09sec, 99.77mph
2nd J. Surtees (MV Agusta) 2h 18m 52.8sec, 97.81mph
3rd R.N. Brown (Gilera) 2h 20m 58.4sec, 96.35mph
4th J. Brett (Norton) 2h 21m 42.8sec, 95.85mph
5th K.R. Campbell (Moto Guzzi) 2h 23m 19.2sec, 94.80mph
6th R.H. Dale (Moto Guzzi) 2h 23m 43.4sec, 94.52mph

Bernard's time for lap six was 25m 21sec

Jack Brett crashed at Sulby on lap seven and was out of the race. He only suffered bruising and blamed the crash on a broken chain. This moved Dickie Dale up to fifth place. Eric Hinton (Norton) also crashed on this lap at Ballacraine; he was in eighth place at the time. Bernard was having an excellent race and had moved up to twelfth position. The leader board after lap seven was:

1st R. McIntyre (Gilera) 2h 39m 12.8sec, 99.54mph
2nd J. Surtees (MV Agusta) 2h 41m 55.8sec, 97.87mph
3rd R.N. Brown (Gilera) 2h 44m 10.4sec, 96.54mph
4th K.R. Campbell (Moto Guzzi) 2h 47m 06.6sec, 94.83mph
5th R.H. Dale (Moto Guzzi) 2h 47m 23.8sec, 94.67mph
6th G.B. Tanner (Norton) 2h 47m 26.6sec, 94.64mph
7th A.J. Trow (Norton) 2h 50m 18sec, 94.12mph
8th A. King (Norton) 2h 51m 12sec, 93.14mph
9th G. Murphy (Matchless) 2h 52m 28sec, 93.10mph
10th J. Buchan (Norton) 2h 53m 21.8sec, 92.32mph
11th R. Barker (Norton) 2h 54m 50sec, 91.43mph
12th B.D. Codd (Norton) 2h 55m 21.8sec, 91.10mph

McIntyre slowed his pace down on the last lap. After receiving signals from Geoff Duke at Sulby of his commanding lead he realised there was no need to push himself or his machine any more than was necessary. His final lap speed was 98.18mph, which was slow in comparison to his previous laps. As a result of this Surtees, still pushing hard, did gain on the leader but McIntyre was always in control. K. Campbell crashed in Ramsey Square when oil leaked onto his rear wheel; however, he remounted and realised he could continue with caution, but he did lose fourth place to Dickie Dale.

Dale was the first rider to cross the line followed by Surtees. McIntyre was next, changing down through his gearbox and slowing down as he did so, knowing he was over two minutes ahead of Surtees. Geoff Tanner had been in contention all race on his Norton but was unlucky on the final lap when his petrol tank split with just five miles to go; he coasted home and finished 28th. The result was:

1st R. McIntyre (Gilera) 3h 02m 57sec, 98.99mph
2nd J. Surtees (MV Agusta) 3h 05m 04.2sec,97.86mph
3rd R.N. Brown (Gilera) 3h 09m 02sec, 95.81mph
4th R.H. Dale (Moto Guzzi) 3h 10m 52.4sec, 94.89mph
5th K.R. Campbell (Moto Guzzi) 3h 14m 10.2sec, 93.27mph
6th A.J. Trow (Norton) 3h 15m 17sec, 92.74mph
7th A. King (Norton) 3h 16m 16sec, 92.27mph
8th G. Murphy (Matchless) 3h 16m 47.6sec, 92.02mph
9th J. Buchan (Norton) 3h 17m 50.6sec, 91.54mph
10th R. Barker (Norton) 3h 19m 29sec, 90.79mph
11th B.D. Codd (Norton) 3h 20m 42sec, 90.24mph
12th F.M. Fox (Norton) 3h 20m 59sec, 90.11mph
Fastest lap of the race: R. McIntyre (Gilera) 22m 23.2sec, 101.12mph

Bernard's fastest lap was his fifth lap 24m 34.8sec

Two other Lincolnshire riders won silver Replicas. They were Peter Davey (Norton) who finished fourteenth with a time of 3h 22m 15.6sec at 89.53mph and George Catlin (Norton) who finished fifteenth with a time of 3h 22m 24.8sec at 89.47mph.

After the race it was reported that the reason Dickie Dale had stopped on the fourth lap was because of a seized piston. He was therefore running on seven cylinders instead of eight, but he still managed to continue to lap with speeds of around 96mph. He didn't mention this to his pit crew when he stopped for fuel because he thought they would retire him from the race. C.F. Salt (BSA) crashed at Ballacraine on the last lap, and unfortunately died of his injuries later in hospital. The "Club Team Award" was won by B.M.C.R.C. (A. Wheeler, 349cc Moto Guzzi, J. Surtees MV Agusta, R. McIntyre Gilera). The "Manufacturer's Team Award" wasn't awarded as no team finished the race intact. Silver Replicas were awarded to the first 19 riders home (time limit of 3h 25m 49sec). Bronze Replicas were awarded to riders in 20th position to 34th position (time limit 3h 39m 32.4sec). The "Jimmy Simpson Trophy", awarded for the fastest lap of the 1957 TT in any event, went to R. McIntyre (Gilera) 101.12mph. The "Visitors Cup" (presented by *The Motorcycle* magazine and awarded to the best performance by a visitor to the British Isles) was won by R.N. Brown (Gilera).

Other results from the 1957 Jubilee TT raced on the 10.79-mile Clypse Circuit are:

Lightweight 125cc TT (10 laps)

1st T. Provini (FB Mondial) 1h 27m 51sec, 73.69mph
2nd C. Ubbiali (MV Agusta) 1h 28m 25sec, 73.22mph
3rd L. Taveri (MV Agusta) 1h 30m 37.8sec, 71.44mph
4th S.H. Miller (FB Mondial) 1h 30m 38.4sec, 71.43mph
5th C.C. Sandford (Mondial) 1h 30m 38.6sec, 71.42mph
6th R. Colombo (MV Agusta) 1h 30m 53sec, 71.24mph
Fastest lap: T. Provini (FB Mondial) 8m 41.8sec, 74.44mph (new record)

Lightweight 250cc TT (10 laps)

1st C.C. Sandford (Mondial) 1h 25m 25.4sec, 75.80mph
2nd L. Taveri (MV Agusta) 1h 27m 12.4sec, 72.24mph
3rd R. Colombo (MV Agusta) 1h 27m 21.8sec, 71.10mph
4th F. Bartos (CZ) 1h 29m 22.4sec, 72.45mph
5th S.H. Miller (FB Mondial) 1h 30m 47sec, 71.31mph
6th D. Chadwick (MV Agusta) 1h 32m 28sec, 70.02mph
Fastest lap: T. Provini (FB Mondial) 8m 18sec, 78mph (new record)
George Catlin (203cc MV Agusta) retired on the fourth lap after posting his fastest lap of the race on the previous lap of 9m 46.2sec

Sidecar TT (10 laps)

1st F. Hillebrand (BMW) 1h 30m 03.4sec, 71.89mph
2nd W. Schneider (BMW) 1h 30m 54.8sec, 71.21mph
3rd F. Camathias (BMW) 1h 32m 18.2sec, 70.14mph
4th J. Beeton (Norton) 1h 36m 40.2sec, 66.97mph
5th C. Freeman (Norton) 1h 39m 53.2sec, 64.82mph
6th P. Woollett (Norton) 1h 41m 50sec, 63.58mph
Fastest lap: F. Hillebrand (BMW) 8m 55.4sec, 72.55mph (new record)

CHAPTER TEN

A TYPICALLY WET CADWELL PARK

"Double win for Codd"

Bernard returned to the mainland after what could only be considered as a reasonably successful International TT. The first meeting on the calendar was Cadwell Park on Sunday 30th June. Rain fell for most of the day for the Whit Monday meeting but despite this the racing was exciting and the spectators that had braved the conditions were not disappointed. The solo classes were dominated by Peter Ferbrache, winning the Senior and Junior events on his Nortons. He excelled in the wet conditions and could lap quicker than any other rider. Even Bernard, George Catlin and Peter Davey, who were all now considered to be Cadwell Park experts, had to give way to his superiority on the day.

There was a mixed entry for the 250cc event, which included eleven different makes of machine including B. Clarke's 242cc Norman Anzani twin and George Catlin on the 203cc MV Agusta. Catlin failed to start the race when his MV Agusta seized on the line. Once D. Pratt (248cc GMV) passed J.F. Patrick (250cc Velocette) he cruised home, a comfortable winner. R. Grey and T. Fenwick on Moto-Guzzis battled for third place with Fenwick emerging the victor.

250cc Solo Final (8 laps)
1st D. Pratt (GMV) 12m 2.02sec, 49.6mph
2nd J.F. Patrick (248cc Velocette)
3rd T.E. Fenwick (248cc Moto Guzzi)
4th R. Grey (247cc Moto Guzzi)

The rain continued to fall steadily during the 350cc heats but the racing continued, the only delay being at the start of the second heat when George Catlin sportingly changed a plug for Bernard on the start line. I can't imagine sportsmanship like that happening in modern-day racing. At the end of the first lap George Catlin (348cc Norton) was leading, closely followed by Bernard. R. Lawrence (BSA) was third and despite some close racing they finished the race in these positions. P. Ferbrache won the third heat.

In the final of the 350cc race George Catlin led after the first lap from R. Lawrence (BSA) second; Bernard was third and P. Ferbrache (348cc Norton) fourth. As they came round the second time Ferbrache clearly had more speed and confidence in the wet conditions and was pressing Bernard. By lap three Ferbrache had passed Bernard and was up to second place. R. Lawrence (BSA) was steadily dropping back. Although Catlin was riding well, P. Ferbrache passed him on lap seven and won by 2.4 seconds. J.A. Sugden passed Bernard on lap five to finish third and demote Bernard to fourth.

350cc Junior Final (8 laps)
1st P. Ferbrache (348cc Norton) 10m 56.6sec, 51.05mph
2nd G. Catlin (348cc Norton)
3rd J.A. Sugden (348cc Norton)
4th B.D. Codd (348cc Norton)

The Sidecar Scratch race was one of the best seen at Cadwell for a long while. J.H.T. Harris (499cc Norton) led from the start but there was a phenomenal battle for second place between Fred Hanks (499cc Norton) and Charlie Freeman (499cc Norton). By the third lap, and after being last to get away at the start, R.A. Robinson on his 996cc Vincent outfit had fought his way up to fourth place. Freeman passed Hanks at Coppice Corner during lap five and the battle for the lead was now between Freeman, Hanks, Harris, and Robinson. Freeman tried to overtake Harris on the last lap on the Mountain bends but was unsuccessful, and Harris won by just two tenths of a second. Only three seconds separated the first five at the line.

Sidecar Scratch Race Final (8 laps)
1st J.T. Harris (499cc Norton) 10m 43.8sec, 51.15mph
2nd C. Freeman (499cc Norton)
3rd F. Hanks (499cc Norton)
4th R.A. Robinson (996cc Vincent)

Peter Ferbrache repeated his earlier win with victory in the 12-lap senior final. George Catlin led for the first six laps but was then passed by Ferbrache at Coppice Hill. Catlin crashed on lap ten while trying to match the pace of the leader, but he had a big enough lead over Bernard in third place that he could rejoin the race and still finish second. Bernard was third and Peter Davey, on a borrowed Norton, fourth.

Unlimited cc Senior Final (12 laps)
1st P. Ferbrache (499cc Norton) 16m 1sec, 56.2mph
2nd G. Catlin (499cc Norton)
3rd B.D. Codd (499cc Norton)
4th P. Davey (499cc Norton)

Sidecar Handicap Final (8 laps)
1st O.E. Greenwood (499cc Norton) 10m 55sec, 51.1mph
2nd R.E. Cheney (499cc Norton)
3rd C. Vincent (499cc BSA)
4th B.L. Gaskin (499cc Norton)

After a wet Cadwell Park it was time for the Cock o' the North meeting at Oliver's Mount, Scarborough on Friday and Saturday, 14th and 15th June. This circuit was not one of Bernard's favourites, probably because he had not been very successful there in the past and this time wasn't to be much better.

Bernard was listed in the programme as riding in the 350cc and 500cc events. There were four seven-lap eliminating heats in the 350cc class, and these were run on the Friday evening.

The meeting started at 9.30am on the Friday with practice until 3.00pm. There were a few incidents during the practice sessions, the most serious being T. Godfrey (348cc Velocette) who crashed when he caught the banking and was thrown over the fencing into a field. He was taken to hospital with a suspected broken collar bone. After the practice period there was a break until the racing started at 5.45pm. At the commencement of each day's racing a rocket was fired, with another rocket fired at the end of the racing to indicate to the spectators when it was safe to go onto the circuit. The first of the 350cc heats was scheduled to start at 6.08pm and the 15-lap final started at 8.24pm, unlike today where there is a noise curfew at many of our racetracks: racing must stop at a certain time at night and can't start until a specified time in the morning because the noise offends people living locally, even though they are aware they are buying a property close to a race circuit! It seems locals didn't mind and didn't object in the 1950s.

Bernard was in the third heat of the 350cc event alongside George Catlin, John Hartle and D.V. Chadwick, all on Nortons. I can't find any reports for these heats, just the names of the winners and their speeds.

350cc Heat Winners (7 laps)
The 16 fastest finishers from the four heats qualified for the final

Heat One
A. King (348cc Norton) 61.2mph £6.00

Heat Two
J. Brett (350cc Norton) 62.02mph £6.00

Heat Three
D.V. Chadwick (350cc Norton) 61.01mph £6.00

Heat Four
R. McIntyre (348cc Norton) 61.75mph £6.00

350cc Final (15 laps)
Winner received The Whitaker Trophy
1st R. McIntyre (348cc Norton) 63.77mph £18.00
2nd J. Brett (350cc Norton) £16.00
3rd D.V. Chadwick (350cc Norton) £14.00
Fastest lap: J. Brett (350cc Norton) 64.84mph £2.00

350cc Scratch Race Final (10 laps)
The 16 second fastest finishers from the four heats qualified for the final
Winner received The Boothby Trophy
1st G.B. Tanner (Norton) 60.67mph £9.00
2nd H. Plews (AJS) £8.00
3rd M.T. Brookes (Norton) £7.00
Fastest lap: G.B. Tanner (Norton) 61.78mph £2.00

In the 500cc class there were three eliminating heats, the first of these starting at 1.41pm on the Saturday. Bernard was in heat two with J. Surtees (Norton), J. Brett (Norton), P.A. Davey (BSA) and A. Shepherd (Norton). The results of the heats were:

500cc Heats (7 laps)

Heat One

The 16 fastest finishers in the three heats qualified for the final

1st P.H. Carter (350cc Norton) 59.60mph £6.00

2nd R. Cousins (499cc Norton) £4.00

3rd L. Carr (498cc Matchless) £3.00

4th T.E. Fenwick (498cc TJS) £2.00

Heat Two

1st J. Surtees (499cc Norton) 64.69mph £6.00

2nd J. Brett (500cc Norton) £4.00

3rd B.D. Codd (499cc Norton) £3.00

4th A. Shepherd (499cc Norton) £2.00

Heat Three

1st R. McIntyre (499cc Norton) 64.09mph £6.00

2nd A. King (499cc Norton) £4.00

3rd G.A. Catlin (499cc Norton) £3.00

4th F. Wallis (499cc BSA) £2.00

The final of the 500cc event was started by Geoff Duke, and from the start looked as if it was going to be a battle between Bob McIntyre and John Surtees, both on Nortons. Surtees posted the fastest lap and had just taken the lead before crashing on the third lap, which left McIntyre to lead for the rest of the race and take the win with J. Brett (Norton) finishing second and A. King (Norton) third. George Catlin (Norton) was fourth and Bernard fifth.

500cc Final (15 laps)

The Winner received The Tesseyman Trophy

1st R. McIntyre (499cc Norton) 65.88mph £20.00

2nd J. Brett (500cc Norton) £18.00

3rd A. King (499cc Norton) £16.00

4th G.A. Catlin (499cc Norton) £14.00

5th B.D. Codd (499cc Norton) £12.00

Fastest lap: J. Surtees (499cc Norton) 66.94mph £2.00

500cc Scratch Final (10 laps)
The 16 second fastest finishers in the three heats qualified for the final
The Winner received The Scarborough Motor Traders Trophy
1st G.T. Salt (499cc Norton) 62.34mph £9.00
2nd P. Ferbrache (Norton) £7.00
3rd G.B. Tanner (500cc Norton) £5.00
Fastest lap: G.T. Salt (499cc Norton) £2.00

250cc Heat Winners (6 laps)
Heat One: J. Surtees (250cc NSU) 59.58mph £6.00
Heat Two: F. Purslow (249cc Triumph) 55.83mph £6.00

250cc Final (12 laps)
Winner received The Jaconelli Trophy
1st J. Surtees (250cc NSU) 60.01mph £15.00
2nd D.V. Chadwick (203cc MV Agusta) £10.00
3rd G. Palmer (249cc PKR Special) £8.00
Fastest lap: J. Surtees (250cc NSU) & D.V. Chadwick (203cc MV Agusta) 61.19mph (new record)

The meeting, which was organised by the Scarborough & District Motor Club Ltd and supported by The Yorkshire Post and The Yorkshire Evening Post, was regarded as a great success. It had attracted a crowd of over 12,000, which was 4,000 more than the same meeting the previous year.

Back to Cadwell Park on June 30th and a chance for Bernard to avenge the defeat he incurred earlier in the month to the dominant Peter Ferbrache in the wet conditions. The weather looked uncertain (as it often does at Cadwell Park), but it didn't deter a reasonably sized crowd from turning out. There were three eight-lap heats in the 350cc class with the first five riders' home in each heat competing in the final. Peter Ferbrache won the first heat. A. Evans won the second and Bernard won the third all riding 348cc Nortons.

In the final, Ferbrache got away first and it looked like it was going to be a repeat of the previous meeting, chased by R. Lawrence (348cc BSA) and Bernard. After two laps Bernard had caught and passed both Lawrence and Ferbrache, much to the delight of the partisan Cadwell crowd. By lap five Ferbrache had claimed back second place but couldn't challenge Bernard for the lead. Bernard went on to win by ten seconds.

350cc Final (8 laps)
1st B.D. Codd (348cc Norton) 9m 53sec, 60.8mph
2nd P. Ferbrache (348cc Norton)
3rd R. Lawrence (348cc BSA)
4th E.R. Fitton (348cc Velocette)

Sidecar Scratch race (8 laps)
1st C. Freeman / T. Leek (499cc Norton) 10m 48sec, 55.5mph
2nd F. Taylor / B. Simpson (499cc Norton)
3rd O.E. Greenwood / T. Fairbrother (499cc Norton)
4th F.C. Pusey / P. Corris (498cc BSA)
Fastest lap: J.H.T. Harris / T. Plant (499cc Norton) 1m 18sec

F. Keeling was the first man away in the all-Norton Sidecar Handicap final with J.T. Harris starting last. Keeling held onto the lead for three laps but then third rider away, E. Cheney, passed him to take the lead. By half race distance Harris was in fifth place, and one lap later he had caught and passed Keeling and was chasing down Cheney and Taylor. In a mad dash out of Barn Corner on the last lap Cheney just managed to stay ahead of Taylor and Harris to take the win.

Sidecar Handicap Final (8 laps)
1st R.E. Cheney / J. Fox (499cc Norton) 11m 42.6sec, 51.4mph
2nd F. Taylor / B. Simpson (499cc Norton)
3rd J.T. Harris / T. Plant (499cc Norton)
4th C. Freeman / T. Leek (499cc Norton)

Lightweight 250cc Solo Final (8 laps)
1st T. Fenwick (248cc Moto-Guzzi) 11m 7sec, 53.9mph
2nd J. Patrick (248cc Velocette)
3rd D. Rose (248cc Velocette)
4th J.R. Worthington (248cc Norton)

This Novice race was for riders who had not competed in any Road Race prior to January 1956 and was sponsored by Mr. Reg Cross who kindly gave awards for the first three riders who finished.

1st A one-piece racing horsehide suit, made to measure
2nd A pair of horsehide boots, made to measure
3rd An approved, stamped A.C.U. racing helmet

The winners of these special awards were:
1st D.W. Phillips (348cc Norton) 10m 21.8sec, 57.5mph
2nd L.A. James (499cc Vincent)
3rd M.T. Brookes (498cc Triumph)

Two heats of the Senior Solo event had very slow times: so slow in fact that sixth place finisher in heat four, Boston rider Stan Cooper (650cc SCS), was fast enough to have won heat two and been second in heat three.

E.R. Fitton (348cc Velocette) surprisingly led the Senior Final race for the first two laps from Ferbrache and Bernard. Ferbrache made his move to the front but not for long; Bernard passed him and consistently increased his lead to win his second final of the day. Ferbrache was second, Middleton (499cc Norton) third and Fitton held on to fourth place.

Senior Solo Final (12 laps)
1st B.D. Codd (499cc Norton) 14m 31.4sec, 62.1mph
2nd P. Ferbrache (499cc Norton)
3rd P. Middleton (499cc Norton)
4th E.R. Fitton (348cc Velocette)
5th H. Plews (499cc Norton)

Harry Plews (499cc Norton) broke the one-lap record in the Senior solo race with a time of 1m 8sec and a speed of 66.18mph. This was eight-tenths of a second quicker than the previous record, which was set by J. Hartle on a works Norton and established at the September meeting of 1956. The headline in the Louth Standard the following week would read "Double win for Codd"

It was announced at this meeting that in the future Bernard would be riding for Gordon Woodman, the Holbeach dealer, and no longer for Les Hallen of Cambridge. Woodman had bought the two 1956 Norton machines (a 348cc and a 499cc model that Bernard had ridden previously) for his rider-mechanic R.H. Lilley to compete on, but Lilley had been injured in a crash at the TT.

Two weeks later, Saturday July 13th, Bernard was competing at the Castle Combe circuit in Wiltshire. The 350cc and 500cc events were run with two eliminating heats and a final. Bernard was in the same heat as Alastair King (Norton) who won the heat with some style, but it was the battle for second place that caught the imagination of the crowd. Bernard came out the eventual victor after a race-long fight with Geoff Tanner (Norton) and D. Minter (Norton).

350cc Heats (5 laps)
Heat One
1st A. King (Norton) 76.70mph
2nd B.D. Codd (Norton)
3rd G. Tanner (Norton)
4th D. Minter (Norton)

Heat Two
1st J.P. Fordham (Norton) 74.76mph

In the 350cc Final, A. King was leading after the first lap with Bernard and Derek Minter in his wheel tracks. At the end of lap two, King had pulled away from Bernard and D. Minter who were racing just inches apart. G. Tanner, P.R. Hodgson (AJS), Alan Rutherford (Duke-BSA) and Jimmy Buchan (Norton) were racing just as closely in the fight for fourth position. By the end of lap four, King was still out in front, and Bernard had pulled away from Minter and was looking set for a second-place finish but then, on lap eight, he was forced to retire with mechanical issues (it was reported later as valve-gear trouble). This left A. King to take a comfortable win with D. Minter second, G. Tanner third, and A. Rutherford finishing fourth.

350cc Final (10 laps)
1st A. King (Norton) 78.81mph
2nd D. Minter (Norton)
3rd G. Tanner (Norton)
4th A. Rutherford (Duke-BSA)
Fastest lap: A. King (Norton) 80.80mph

500cc Heats (5 laps)
Heat One
1st G. *Murphy (Matchless) 77.42mph*

Heat Two
1st D. *Minter (Norton) 80.51mph*

In the Final of the 500cc race Bernard got a good start and led the race from A. King. D. Minter was third and J. Buchan fourth. As they crossed the line to complete the second lap, King was just inches ahead of Bernard, Minter was still third, but Tanner had passed Buchan to take fourth place. At the end of the next lap Bernard was back in the lead. Then, as the five riders rounded Camp Corner to go onto the home straight to start their fourth lap, A. King made a mistake, went onto the grass, and re-joined in fourth place behind Tanner, Bernard, and Minter. By the sixth lap King had closed the gap and was up with the leaders again and in doing so broke the lap record with a speed of 85.79mph, but he couldn't get the better of Tanner who went on to win. It is not certain what happened to Bernard after he was involved in this tussle for the lead, but he isn't mentioned any more in any report I can find.

500cc Final (12 laps)
1st G.B. Tanner (Norton) 82.16mph
2nd A. King (Norton)
3rd D. Minter (Norton)
Fastest lap: A. King (Norton) 85.79mph (record)

C. Smith (Norton), current lap record holder R.A. Robinson (998cc Vincent) and B. Boddice (Norton) lined up for the Sidecar Scratch race. Robinson set a fast pace from the start but couldn't get away from Boddice and Smith. On lap four Smith took the lead and slowly increased his advantage until the chequered flag.

Sidecar Scratch race Final (8 laps)
1st C. Smith (Norton) 75.17mph
2nd W.G. Boddice (Norton)
3rd R.A. Robinson (998cc Vincent)
Fastest lap: C. Smith (Norton) 77.94mph

Sidecar Handicap race Final (8 laps)
1st G.D. Payne (Norton-Triumph) 68.29mph
2nd P.J. Millard (Norton)
3rd F. Keeling (Norton)
Fastest lap: C. Smith (Norton) & L. Taylor (Norton) 76.15mph

The Lightweight (125cc) Final was won by J. Baughn (MV Agusta).

Lightweight 125cc Final (5 laps)
1st J. Baughn (MV Agusta) 67.59mph
2nd D.H. Edlin (MV Agusta)
3rd D.C. Moore (MV Agusta)
Fastest lap: J. Baughn (MV Agusta) 70.48mph (new record)

In the 250cc event J. Baughn rode a Moto-Guzzi. He made a bad start and was fourth at the end of lap one but fought his way through the field to lead on lap four and from then on he steadily increased his lead to win comfortably. P. Tait (Beasley-Velocette) won the three-way battle for second place with J. Hamilton (NSU) and S.M.B. Hailwood (MV Agusta).

250cc Final (6 laps)
1st J. Baughn (Moto Guzzi) 69.74mph
2nd P.H. Tait (Beasley-Velocette)
3rd J.D. Hamilton (NSU)
4th S.M.B. Hailwood (MV Agusta)
Fastest lap: P.H. Tait (Beasley-Velocette) 73.10mph

Non-experts 350cc Heats (5 laps)

Heat One
1st J.D. Hamilton (AJS) 73.57mph

Heat Two
1st L.G. Hodgson (AJS) 73.90mph

Non-experts 350cc Final (8 laps)
1st L.G. Hodgson (AJS) 75.04mph
2nd R. Thompson (Norton)
3rd O.P. Williams (Norton)
Fastest lap: L.G. Hodgson (AJS) 77.04mph

Non-experts 1000cc Heats (5 laps)

Heat One
1st M.A. Bowdrey (Norton) 76.17mph

Heat Two
1st J. Clarke (Norton) 74.63mph
Non-experts 1000cc Final (8 laps)
1st J. Clarke (Norton) 75.75mph
2nd M.A. Bowdrey (Norton)
3rd K.W. Douglas (BSA)
Fastest lap: R. Thompson (Norton) 80.19mph

The following day, Sunday July 14th, Bernard was at a wet Snetterton meeting where the battles of the previous day between Geoff Tanner, Derek Minter, and Bernard - all on Nortons - continued.

The persistent rain eased just before the racing started at 1.30pm but the track was slow to dry out. The 125cc race was the first event on the programme and saw D.H. Edlin and J. Baughn, both on MV Agustas, fight for the lead just a few feet apart. John Hogan (MV Agusta) moved up to third place on the second lap after a bad start but, in trying to match the pace of the leading riders, he crashed on lap three at Riches Corner and injured his arm. J. Baughn passed Edlin soon after and won by over 20 yards. Mike Hailwood (MV Agusta) was third.

125cc solo Race (4 laps)
1st J. Baughn (MV Agusta) 64.97mph
2nd D.H. Edlin (MV Agusta)
3rd S.M.B. Hailwood (MV Agusta)
Fastest lap: J. Baughn (MV Agusta) 68.15mph

In the 250cc race J. Hogan was riding his 203cc MV Agusta despite his injury from the previous race. He again got a bad start but fought his way up to fifth place before retiring with mechanical trouble on lap five. Mike Hailwood (204cc MV Agusta) had taken the lead on the third lap and consistently increased his lead to win with T. Thorp (BSA) second and D. Shorey (Norvel) third.

250cc solo Race (6 laps)
1st S.M.B. Hailwood (204cc MV Agusta) 68.53mph
2nd T. Thorp (BSA)
3rd D. Shorey (Norvel)
Fastest lap: J. Hogan (203cc MV Agusta)72.53mph

The track was almost dry for the 350cc heats. The first heat was won by J. Lewis (Norton) with Geoff Tanner (Norton) second. Bernard won the second heat after a battle with D. Minter (Norton)

350cc Heats (7 laps)
Heat One
1st J. Lewis (Norton) 78.22mph

Heat Two
1st B.D. Codd (Norton) 78.01mph

In the final of the 350cc event D. Minter led from the start but crashed out at Coram Curve on the first lap when he lost control of his Norton on a still-damp surface. R.H. King (Norton) had made a phenomenal start and now led G. Tanner (Norton) and A. Rutherford (Duke-BSA) until he was passed by Tanner on lap three. Bernard had made a terrible start and it took him until lap five to catch and pass Rutherford. By the start of the final lap Bernard was closing in on King and passed him at Riches Corner to take second place. Tanner had pulled a good lead by now and looked certain to win but Bernard caught him and seemed to have a quicker line through the 'Esses', managing to overtake him and, as he crossed the finish line, he was pulling away from Tanner.

350cc solo Final (10 laps)
1st B.D. Codd (Norton) 69.78mph
2nd G.B. Tanner (Norton)
3rd R.H. King (Norton)
Fastest lap: B.D. Codd (Norton) 74.07mph

P.V. "Pip" Harris (Norton) dominated the two sidecar races with J. Beeton (Norton) achieving two podiums.

500cc Sidecar Race (6 laps)
1st P.V. Harris (Norton) 71.02mph
2nd E. Walker (Norton)
3rd J. Beeton (Norton)
Fastest lap: P.V. Harris (Norton) 72.31mph

1200cc Sidecar Race (6 laps)
1st P.V. Harris (Norton) 77.47mph
2nd P. Robinson (998cc Vincent)
3rd J. Beeton (Norton)
Fastest lap: P.V. Harris (Norton) 81.00mph

500cc Heats (7 laps)
Heat One
1st E. Washer (Norton) 76.33mph

Heat Two
1st B.D. Codd (Norton) 79.77mph

The 500cc Final saw Bernard and J. Buchan (Norton) contesting the lead from the start. If G. Tanner (Norton) had remembered to turn his petrol on he would undoubtedly have been challenging for the lead as well, but he lost too much time and never recovered. Buchan led for two laps before Bernard passed him and led for the next lap, only to be overtaken by Buchan who then led for four laps and looked to have the upper hand. Bernard kept in Buchan's slipstream and squeezed through on the approach to Riches Corner and then pulled away slightly. Buchan tried everything he knew but didn't worry Bernard anymore. Bernard won by about 50 yards. J. Payne (Norton) and P. Ferbrache (Norton) battled for third place all through the race, constantly swapping places with D. Minter close behind. On the last lap Minter slipped past Payne to finish fourth.

500cc solo Final (10 laps)
1st B.D. Codd (Norton) 83.46mph
2nd J. Buchan (Norton)
3rd P. Ferbrache (Norton)
4th D. Minter (Norton)
Fastest lap: B.D. Codd (Norton) 86.02mph

So, another double win for Bernard - once more against quality opposition - showing he certainly had the ability given the right machinery. The Standard on Friday 8th August reported this meeting and remarked that "*the Nortons he is now riding for Gordon Woodman of Holbeach seem to have more urge than those he competed on earlier in the season*".

Oulton Park on Saturday August 3rd was the next outing for Bernard riding Gordon Woodman's Nortons. This was a combination of rider, machine and sponsor that seemed to be working as well as the legendary Munks/Coupland combination of the early days. In saying that this was not a successful meeting for Bernard, the only time I can find his name mentioned in any report is in the 500cc final when it states that he was fighting with K.H. Patrick (Norton) for fifth position and these two provided the excitement in what was otherwise an uneventful race. Nevertheless, I have included the results of the day.

50cc Solo Final (3 laps)
1st F.W. Launchbury (49cc Itom) 9m 20.2sec, 52.94mph
2nd S.M.B. Hailwood (49cc Itom)
3rd C.V. Dawson (49cc Itom)
4th F. Sheene (49cc Astor-Special)
Fastest lap: F.W. Launchbury (49cc Itom) 3m 5.4sec, 53.61mph

1200cc Sidecar Championship (8 laps)
1st P.V. Harris (499cc Norton) 17m 15.6sec, 76.63mph
2nd C. Smith (499cc Norton)
3rd W.G. Boddice (499cc Norton)
4th R.A. Robinson (998cc Vincent- Special)
Fastest lap: P.V. Harris (499cc Norton) 2m 7.2sec, 78.14mph

125cc Solo Championship Final (8 laps)
1st C.C. Sandford (125cc Mondial) 17m 54sec, 73.89mph
2nd D.H. Edlin (124cc MV Agusta)
3rd S.M.B. Hailwood (124cc MV Agusta)
4th W.M. Webster (124cc MV Agusta)
Fastest lap: C.C. Sandford (125cc Mondial) 2m 11.6sec, 75.53mph
(new record) (Lambretta Trophy)

250cc Championship Final (10 laps)
1st C.C. Sandford (250cc Mondial) 20m 54.4sec, 79.11mph
2nd J. Surtees (247cc NSU)
3rd R.N. Brown (247cc NSU)
4th J.D. Hamilton (247cc NSU)
Fastest lap: C.C. Sandford (250cc Mondial) 2m 02.6sec, 81.07mph
(new record)

In posting the fastest lap in the 250cc event C.C. Sandford won the Sir Algernon Guinness Memorial Trophy. This was awarded to the rider who improved the lap record in any class by the greatest margin. Sandford previously held the lap record which he established on a 248cc Moto Guzzi. His new record was 1.70mph faster.

350cc Heats
Heat One
1st J. Surtees (348cc Norton)

Heat Two
1st J. Hartle (348cc Norton)

Heat Three
1st D.V. Chadwick (Norton)

350cc Championship Final (12 laps)
1st J. Surtees (348cc Norton) 24m 17.6sec, 81.71mph
(Slazenger Challenge Cup)
2nd G.A. Murphy (348cc AJS)
3rd J. Brett (348cc Norton)
4th A. King (348cc Norton)
Fastest lap: J. Hartle (348cc Norton) 1m 58.4sec, 83.95mph (new record)

Sidecar Handicap Race (8 laps)
1st P.J. Millard (499cc Norton) 19m 16.6sec, 70.43mph
2nd D.H. Saywood (Norton)
3rd B.G. Gross (499cc Norton)
4th E.T. Young (ETY-Triumph)
Fastest lap: P.V. Harris (499cc Norton) 2m 05.6sec, 79.14mph (new record)

Up to 1000cc Championship Heat Winners:

Heat One
1st J. Surtees (500cc MV Agusta)

Heat Two
1st A. King (499cc Norton)

Heat Three
1st R. Fay (499cc Norton)

Up to 1000cc Championship Final (12 laps)
1st J. Surtees (500cc MV Agusta) 23m 17sec, 85.26mph
2nd A. King (499cc Norton)
3rd J. Brett (499cc Norton)
4th R. Fay (499cc Norton)
Fastest lap: J. Surtees (500cc MV Agusta) 1m 55.2sec, 86.29mph
(new record)

This was the fastest lap of the day and therefore John Surtees won the Hector Dugdale Trophy. The previous record was held by Geoff Duke with a speed of 85.69mph. So, five new lap records in the seven events, but not a good day for Bernard and the Gordon Woodman Team.

Two days later, on Bank Holiday Monday August 5th, Cadwell Park was the venue for the next meeting, which was a National Road Race event for Solo, Sidecar and 500cc Cars and organised by The Louth & District Motorcycle Club.

The first event of the day was the Lightweight race for solo machines under 250cc. A.G. Briggs (199cc Triumph) got a blistering start but was in third place at the end of the first lap behind J. Murgatroyd (248cc Velocette) and J.F. Patrick (248cc Velocette). Murgatroyd went on to win and was only challenged by P. Tomes (248cc J.E.L.) who, after a bad start, battled his way through the field from sixth place on the first lap to finish second. John Hartle was unable to start this race as he had damaged his 248cc MV Agusta in a crash the previous day at Oulton Park.

250cc Lightweight Race (8 laps)
1st J. Murgatroyd (248cc Velocette) 10m 45sec, 56.05mph £10.00
2nd P. Tomes (248cc J.E.L.) 10m 46.5sec £7.00
3rd J.F. Patrick (248cc Velocette) 10m 55.8sec £4.00
4th D. Rose (248cc Velocette) 10m 59sec £3.00
5th D. Pratt (248cc (G.M.V.) 11m 1sec £2.00
6th T.E. Fenwick (248cc Moto Guzzi) 11m 2.5sec £1.00

P. Ferbrache (348cc Norton) won the first eliminating heat of the 350cc Junior Race with J.A. Sugden (348cc Norton) second and Peter Davey (348cc Norton) third.

350cc Junior Race Heats (6 laps)
First 7 in each heat qualified for the final

Heat One
1st P. Ferbrache (348cc Norton)
2nd J.A. Sugden (348cc Norton)
3rd P.A. Davey (348cc Norton)
4th L.P. Young (349cc AJS)
5th P.D. Chatterton (348cc Norton)

Bernard was in heat two alongside J. Hartle (348cc Norton) and established a commanding first lap lead that Hartle could only slowly reduce and, in keeping ahead of the challenge from Hartle, Bernard set a new six-lap record of 7m 22sec, which improved his own previous record of 7m 25sec by three seconds. This he posted at the September meeting 1956. In chasing Bernard, J. Hartle set a new one-lap record of 1m 10.5sec and was just half a second behind when they crossed the line.

Heat Two
1st B.D. Codd (348cc Norton) 7m 22sec
2nd J. Hartle (348cc Norton) 7m 22.5sec
3rd J.B. Denton (348cc BSA) 7m 46sec
4th R. Lawrence (348cc BSA) 7m 47sec
5th P. Minion (348cc BSA) 7m 57sec
6th P. Middleton (348cc Norton)

In the final of the 350cc event John Hartle took the lead and held it to the flag, Bernard was second throughout the race but was always losing ground on the leader. Hartle set a new eight lap record of 9m 41.4sec; the previous record was 9m 46sec and was held by Peter Murphy on a 348cc AJS.

350cc Junior Final (8 laps)
1st J. Hartle (348cc Norton) 9m 41.4sec (new record) £20.00
2nd B.D. Codd (348cc Norton) £12.00
3rd P. Ferbrache (348cc Norton) £10.00

4th P. Davey (348cc BSA) £5.00
5th R. Lawrence (348cc BSA) £3.00
6th J.B. Denton (348cc BSA) £2.00
Fastest lap: J. Hartle (348cc Norton) 1m 10.8sec, 64.05mph

Sidecar Scratch Race Heats (6 laps)
First five in each heat qualified for the final
Heat One
1st R.A. Robinson / L.P. Young (998cc Vincent) 8m7sec
2nd O.E. Greenwood / T. Fairbrother (499cc Norton) 8m 11.5sec
3rd E. Walker / D. Roberts (499cc Norton) 8m 23sec
4th P.E. Russell / B. Silk (499cc Norton) 8m 24.5sec
5th R.E. Cheney / J. Fox (499cc Norton) 8m 24.8sec

In heat two of the Sidecar Scratch event C. Smith (499cc Norton) broke the existing one-lap record, which was held by Bill Boddice and set at the September meeting 1956, by 1.2 seconds.

Heat Two
1st C. Smith / E. Bliss (499cc Norton) 9m 41.4sec
2nd M.J. Youell / T. Cook (499cc Norton)
3rd F.C. Pusey / Unknown (499cc Norton)
4th S.W. Rycroft / G. Deakin (499cc Matchless)

Sidecar Scratch Final (8 laps)
1st R.A. Robinson / L.P. Young (998cc Vincent) 10m 29.6sec, 57.05mph £40.00
2nd C. Smith / E. Bliss (499cc Norton) 10m 16.8sec, £20.00
3rd O.E. Greenwood / T. Fairbrother (499cc Norton) 10m 30.5sec, £12.00
4th E. Walker / D. Roberts (499cc Norton) 11m 0.6sec, £6.00
5th R.E. Cheney / J. Fox (499cc Norton) 11m 1sec, £4.00
6th M.J. Youell / T. Cook (499cc Norton) £2.00
Fastest lap: C. Smith (499cc Norton) 1m 16sec, 59.21mph (new record)

The Sidecar Handicap Race was run in two parts with the best times from each race counting for the result. Part two of the event provided the most entertainment as the first four outfits to cross the line were all within a few seconds of each other.

Sidecar Handicap Race Final Placings (8 laps)
1st E. Walker / D. Roberts (499cc Norton) 11m 4.5sec
2nd R.E. Cheney / J. Fox (499cc Norton)
3rd C. Freeman / J. Ceisnell (499cc Norton)
4th R.A. Robinson / L.P. Young (998cc Vincent)

The main event of the day was the Coronation Trophy, which was for solo machines from 251cc to 1000cc. There were three heats, with the first five in each heat qualifying for the final.

Coronation Trophy Heats (6 laps)
Heat One
1st K.H. Patrick (499cc Norton) 7m 34.8sec
2nd J. Stancer (499cc Norton)
3rd A. Evans (499cc Norton)
4th J.B. Denton (348cc BSA)
5th R.A. Rowbottom (499cc Norton)

Heat Two
1st J. Hartle (499cc Norton) 7m 19sec (new record)
2nd B.D. Codd (499cc Norton) 7m 19.1sec
3rd P. Ferbrache (499cc Norton) 7m 33.5sec
4th N.H. Storer (499cc BSA)
5th L. Carr (498cc Matchless)

Bernard pushed John Hartle all the way in the second heat of the Coronation Trophy Race. Hartle led the first lap with Bernard not getting the best of starts, but once Bernard settled down and got into a rhythm he was never very far behind. In pressing Hartle it resulted in another lap record for Hartle of 7m 19sec with Bernard just one-tenth of a second slower, both riders beating the existing record of 7m 19.2sec, which was held by J. Hartle and again set at the September 1956 meeting.

Heat Three
1st P. Middleton (499cc Norton) 7m 23.5sec,
2nd R. Cousins (499cc Norton) 7m 30sec
3rd P.A. Davey (499cc Norton) 7m 48sec
4th Stan Cooper (650cc S.C.S.)
5th J.R. Holder (499cc Norton)

The Final of the Coronation Trophy was a relatively easy win for John Hartle, as he led from start to finish with P. Middleton in second place for the first six laps before Bernard, after another poor start, caught and passed him at the bottom of Coppice Hill. P. Davey (499cc Norton) was wheel-to-wheel with K.H. Patrick (499cc Norton) fighting for fifth place until, just after passing Davey, Patrick retired with mechanical issues on lap fourteen. J. Hartle's best lap was 1m 8sec, which equates to a speed of 66.18mph and equalled the existing lap record. His time for eight laps smashed the previous eight-lap record by six seconds. Bernard and P. Middleton were also under the previous record time. The result was:

Coronation Trophy Final (20 laps)

1st J. Hartle (499cc Norton) 23m 28.2sec, (£100.00) & Coronation Trophy
2nd B.D. Codd (499cc Norton) 23m 34sec, £50.00
3rd P. Middleton (499cc Norton) 23m 56.5sec, £25.00
4th P. Ferbrache (499cc Norton) 24m 5.4sec, £12.00
5th P.A. Davey (499cc Norton) 24m 30.8sec, £6.00
6th R. Cousins (499cc Norton) 24m 36sec, £3.00

It was at this meeting that Jack Pitcher of Wrangle recorded his first win of his racing career when he won the 500cc Car Handicap Race driving his 499cc Cooper-Norton. His winning time was 10m 35.9sec for the ten-lap race. R.A.R. Bell (499cc Cooper-Norton) was second and R.T. Spreckley (499cc Cooper-Norton) third.

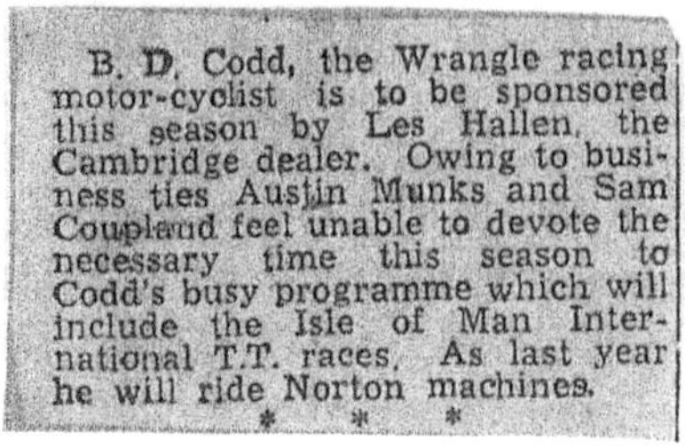

B. D. Codd, the Wrangle racing motor-cyclist is to be sponsored this season by Les Hallen, the Cambridge dealer. Owing to business ties Austin Munks and Sam Coupland feel unable to devote the necessary time this season to Codd's busy programme which will include the Isle of Man International T.T. races. As last year he will ride Norton machines.

* * *

Newspaper cutting from
The Cambridge Daily News
7th March, 1957

Mallory Park programme
14th April, 1957

Snetterton programme
21st April, 1957

Oulton Park programme
22nd April, 1957

In the paddock at Oulton Park
22nd April, 1957

Castle Combe programme
27th April, 1957

Mallory Park programme
12th May, 1957

Bernard's bike in the
paddock at Mallory Park
12th May, 1957

North West 200 programme
18th May, 1957

Jubilee TT programme
and Official Guide

Before the start of the
Junior TT 1957

Pushing up to the start line
for the Junior TT 1957

Going well in the Junior TT 1957 until he had to retire on lap seven

Senior TT 1957

Bernard finished eleventh behind R. Barker (No 67) in the Senior TT 1957

Scarborough programme
14th -15th June, 1957

CADWELL PARK

Midsummer Road Races - Sunday, June 30, 12.30 p.m.

100 solos and 20 sidecars including Bernard Codd, Pete Ferbrache, G. Catlin, B. Denton, E. R. Fitton, H. Plews, etc.

Sidecars: Fred Hanks, John Harris, Frank Taylor, O. E. Greenwood, M. G. Youell, C. Freeman (all Nortons), C. Bailey (600 B.M.W.), C. Vincent and F. Pusey (B.S.As), etc.

Organised by Louth and District M.C.C.

Cadwell Park advertisement
for 30th June, 1957

Cadwell Park programme
30th June, 1957

Cadwell Park advertisement for
August Bank Holiday Meeting

Cadwell Park August Bank Holiday
Monday programme, 1957

Bernard chasing John Hartle over the mountain
at Cadwell Park August Bank Holiday

Bernard at home
with his impressive
trophy collection
in the 1950s

CHAPTER ELEVEN

CRYSTAL PALACE

"In the first 50 yards that I had gone he had gone 150"

After what must have been a disappointing meeting at Oulton Park, Bernard travelled to Crystal Palace for the first time on 17th August. The event was organised by the British Motorcycle Racing Club (BMCRC) on behalf of the London County Council. John Surtees dominated in the three classes he entered - the 250cc, 350cc and Senior Championship races - but he was not the only quality rider Bernard was up against: Derek Minter, Alastair King, Peter Ferbrache and Geoff Tanner were also there, so it was not going to be easy but, no doubt Bernard was quietly confident.

In the two years Bernard had been Road Racing he had not just acquired knowledge of the circuits he raced at but also invaluable knowledge of the riders he raced against. John Surtees was probably the most successful rider of the time, and always seemed to have the advantage of getting a phenomenal start and had sometimes won the race by the time he reached the first corner. Bernard had studied Surtees on the start line on several occasions and, in an interview years later, explained what he had deduced:

> *"I'd watched John Surtees for several years, and if you watched him when the flag dropped, Surtees would be pushing first. He used to watch for a flicker of the starters arm, I'm sure he did, instead of the flag, because he was always pushing first! One day I decided not to watch the flag. Instead, I watched him out of the corner of my eye. When he started pushing, I started pushing. In the first 50 yards that I had gone he had gone 150! It was like trying to race an Austin Seven against a Jag."*

The first event was the heats for the 251cc to 350cc. Bernard was in heat one but, unfortunately, the programme is not completed, and I can only say that A. King (348cc Norton) won the heat, R.H. King (348cc Norton) was fourth and F.J. Stevens (348cc BSA) finished fifth. There is no mention of Bernard, but he didn't qualify for the final. The heat results were:

251cc to 350cc Heats (5 laps)
Heat One
The fastest 24 to finish in the three heats qualified for the final
1st A. King (348cc Norton) 70.00mph
2nd unknown
3rd unknown
4th R.H. King (348cc Norton)
5th F.J. Stevens (348cc BSA)

Heat Two
1st J.R. Clark (348cc Norton) 69.76mph
2nd D.W. Minter (348cc Norton)
3rd F.G. Perris (348cc Norton)
4th P.R. Hodgson (348cc AJS)
5th R. Lawrence (348cc BSA)

Heat Three
1st J. Surtees (348cc Norton) 72.43mph
2nd G.A. Murphy (349cc AJS)
3rd P. Ferbrache (348cc Norton)
4th G.B. Tanner (348cc Norton)
5th R.S. Dixon (349cc Velocette)

251cc to 350cc Final (15 laps)
1st J. Surtees (348cc Norton) 74.79mph
2nd G.A. Murphy (349cc AJS)
3rd A. King (348cc Norton)
4th D.W. Minter (348cc Norton)
5th G.B. Tanner (348cc Norton)
6th P. Ferbrache (348cc Norton)
7th F.G. Perris (348cc Norton)
8th D.V. Chadwick (348cc Norton)
9th T. Thorp (348cc Norton)
10th R. Lawrence (348cc BSA)
11th F.A. Rutherford (Duke-BSA)
12th K.E. Tully (348cc Norton)
Fastest lap J. Surtees (348cc Norton) 76.51mph (new record)

50cc Final (3 laps)
1st F.W.J. Launchbury (49.5cc Itom) 50.21mph
2nd C.V. Dawson (49.5cc Itom)
3rd R.R. Dendy (50cc Dendy-Ducati)
Fastest lap: F.W.J. Launchbury (49.5cc Itom) 51.8mph

125cc Final (8 laps)
1st D.V. Chadwick (123.5cc MV Agusta)65.58mph
2nd D.C. Moore (123.5cc MV Agusta)
3rd J. Baughn (125cc MV Agusta)
Fastest lap: D.V. Chadwick (123.5cc MV Agusta) 68.17mph

250cc Final (12 laps)
1st J. Surtees (250cc NSU) 72.45mph
2nd R.M. Harding (249cc Velocette)
3rd T. Thorp (249cc BSA)
Fastest lap: J. Surtees (250cc NSU) 74.24mph

Sidecar Championship Heats (5 laps)
The fastest eight riders to finish in the two heats qualified for the final

Heat One
1st W.G. Boddice / W. Canning (499cc Norton) 67.91mph
2nd J. Beeton / E.C. Bulgin (499cc Norton)
3rd B.N. Green / W. Rushmere (499cc Norton)
4th F.J. Swindells / B. Bliss (499cc Norton)
5th F. Hanks / E. Dorman (499cc Norton)
6th E.T. Young / C.D. Young (498cc E.T.Y.-Triumph)
7th D.H. Saywood / L.T. White (499cc Norton)
8th G.D. Payne / R. Studer (498cc Norton-Triumph)

Heat Two
1st P.V. Harris / R. Campbell (499cc Norton) 68.32mph
2nd A Young / AC Partridge (499cc Norton)
3rd L Wells / A McKone (499cc WR Norton)
4th LW Taylor / P Glover (499cc Norton)
5th E Walker / DG Roberts (499cc Norton)
6th PJ Millard / S Teather (499cc Norton)
7th BG Gross / RG Douglas (499cc Norton)
8th RJ Ireland / J Warburton (497cc Norton-JAP)

Sidecar Championship Final (12 laps)
1st P.V. Harris / R. Campbell (499cc Norton) 69.92mph
2nd J. Beeton / E.C. Bulgin (499cc Norton)
3rd A. Young / A.C. Partridge (499cc Norton)
4th W.G. Boddice / W. Canning (499cc Norton)
5th F. Hanks / E. Dorman (499cc Norton)
6th B.N. Green / W. Rushmere (499cc Norton)
Fastest lap: P.V. Harris (499cc Norton) 71.9mph

351cc to 1000cc Senior Championship Race Heats (5 laps)
The fastest 24 riders to finish in the two 1000cc heats qualified for the Final

Heat One
1st J. Surtees (500cc Norton)74.03mph
2nd D.W. Minter (499cc Norton)
3rd G.A. Murphy (498cc Matchless)

Bernard was in the second heat of the 1000cc Senior Championship event and was hoping to qualify for the final after the disappointment of failing to qualify for the 350cc final earlier. His race started well, he was with a group of riders and was in sixth place after the first lap; on the second lap he had moved up to fourth place and was going well, optimistic of getting a good grid position for the final. New Zealand rider J.G. Hempleman was in fifth place when Bernard grounded his footrest; as he was getting his Norton under control, the front wheel of Hempleman's bike hit the rear wheel of Bernard's Norton bringing them both down. Bernard slid into the unprotected railway sleepers that lined the track and, as a result, shattered his right thigh bone. Hempleman suffered a broken collar bone. Bernard was taken to Beckenham Hospital in Kent.

Unlike modern-day motorcycle racing the safety precautions in the 1950s were very primitive and, at times, non-existent; the tracks were lined with railway sleepers, oil drums and - if you were lucky - straw bales, and these were in place to define track limits more than as a safety feature. These days there is inflatable air fencing, Recticel safety barriers, gravel traps to slow the bikes down and run-off areas to make the sport a lot safer. Riders also have inflatable airbags in their leathers that are automatically activated when they crash, but this was in a time before Health & Safety existed in the capacity it does now, and if you crashed you took your chances. The race continued and the result was:

Heat Two
1st P. Ferbrache (499cc Norton) 73.59mph
2nd A. King (499cc Norton)

351cc to 1000cc Senior Championship Final (15 laps)
1st J. Surtees (500cc Norton) 77.17mph
2nd D.W. Minter (499cc Norton)
3rd A. King (499cc Norton)
Fastest lap: J. Surtees (500cc Norton) 79.43mph (new record)

So, Saturday August 17th, 1957, was not necessarily a day that stands out in the memory for many people: Elvis Presley was number one in the charts with "All Shook Up", Robin Cousins, the British figure skater and 1980 Olympic gold medallist was born, and Harold Macmillan was Conservative Prime Minister. Just an ordinary August day but, if you are old enough and were a motorcycle racing fan at the time, you will probably recall that this was the day that Bernard raced at Crystal Palace and had his career-ending crash.

By this stage of Bernard's racing career things were looking promising: he had some competitive machinery, a good sponsor, and he had proved that on his day he could compete with - and beat - the best international riders in the sport who were often on superior motorcycles. In the two years that Bernard had been racing he had won two Clubman TTs, numerous short-circuit races across the country and had a trophy cabinet to be proud of. He also set records that can never be surpassed, and no-one can argue that if it hadn't had been for this unfortunate accident and the long-term problems that followed because of the injury Bernard Codd's name would be as recognisable in motorcycling history as Bob McIntyre, Geoff Duke, and John Surtees.

At the time, Austin Munks - the man who played a major part in Bernard's early success - was negotiating with the Italian manufacturer Gilera (as he had done for Geoff Duke in 1953) for Bernard to ride for them in 1958. Unfortunately, this would not have materialised anyway, as Gilera withdrew from racing at the end of 1957 saying it was down to expenditures. Giuseppe Gilera had revealed that the 1957 season had cost 200 million Lire and he considered this to be a very expensive way of advertising. The reality was that since Giuseppe Gilera's only son Ferruccio had died, the racing side of the Gilera factory had lost its way somewhat as he had been in control of the racing department. Gilera did, however, return to racing a few years later.

I'm sure there would have been other factory teams that would have seen Bernard's potential and have shown the same interest in him as Gilera had, and who can say how Bernard's future would have transpired?

CHAPTER TWELVE

THE LONG ROAD TO RECOVERY

"I may have a go at 500cc Car Racing"

Bernard's parents visited him on the Sunday at Beckenham Hospital and were pleased to find him quite cheerful under the circumstances. At this point it was expected that he would be in hospital for the next three months, so he had accepted he would not be racing any more that season.

At first, his leg was put in a splint but, after spending two months in Beckenham Hospital, there was very little improvement. Eventually it was discovered that the bones in Bernard's leg were not fusing together easily so an operation was performed, and a steel pin inserted to assist the join. Three weeks later, on Sunday 20th October he was sent home and told to rest his leg for twelve months. While he was at home, he started to take a few steps with the aid of crutches and continued treatment as an outpatient at Boston Hospital. He remained optimistic and hoped to make a full recovery. Bernard and his family told the Standard they were grateful to all the people who had shown concern after the accident and had enquired about his progress.

Apparently, if you were to suffer the same injury today Doctors would advise you to keep the damaged joint mobile so with Bernard resting his leg it stiffened up and left him with no movement in his knee joint at all.

Bernard's recovery being slow, Dickie Dale recommended he went to see Doctor Galloway, a surgeon at the South Middlesex Hospital. He took Dale's advice and when Doctor Galloway examined his leg it was discovered that, during the healing process, bone callous had fused with muscle tissue, which was preventing him regaining any movement. Bernard had thirteen operations in a short period of time but, although he did regain some movement in his knee joint, it was clear that he would never have enough flexibility to enable him to race motorcycles again.

There was a newspaper report on March 5th, 1958, that stated Bernard was still on crutches and would certainly not be back racing motorcycles this season. It went on to say that the movement in his knee joint was limited and because the break was just three inches above his knee Doctors confirmed he would never be able to get 90 degrees of movement in it. If this was to be the end of his motorcycle racing career, Bernard told the Standard, *"I may have a go at 500cc car racing".*

While Bernard was convalescing, the Louth & District Motorcycle Club celebrated their Silver Jubilee year by staging a larger-than-usual annual dinner and dance at Louth Town Hall. Guest of Honour was Graham Walker: ex-TT winner, former editor of "Motorcycling" magazine and motorcycle racing broadcaster. Other guests, past trophy winners and record holders included Tommy Wood, George Brown, Eric Oliver, Ernie Proctor, Tommy Bateman, George Oliver, Harry Frow, Jack Beeton, and Freddie Frith the Club President. In his speech Freddie Frith praised Bernard and named him in his topflight riders, and as one of the experts of the Cadwell Park Circuit. Although Bernard was invited there is no mention in the report of him attending the evening.

Crystal Palace programme for 17th August, 1957

LONDON COUNTY COUNCIL
CRYSTAL PALACE

Nº 28

ADMIT CAR AND FIVE OCCUPANTS

TERRACE CAR PARK £1 INNER CIRCUIT

(*Including Entertainment Tax*)

SATURDAY, 17th AUGUST, 1957

MOTOR CYCLE RACING

FOR CONDITIONS SEE OVER

NOT TRANSFERABLE NO RE-ADMISSION

NO MONEY REFUNDED IN ANY CIRCUMSTANCES

THIS LABEL MUST BE, AND REMAIN, GUMMED TO THE WINDSCREEN

P.T.O.

Crystal Palace ticket

Crystal Palace poster

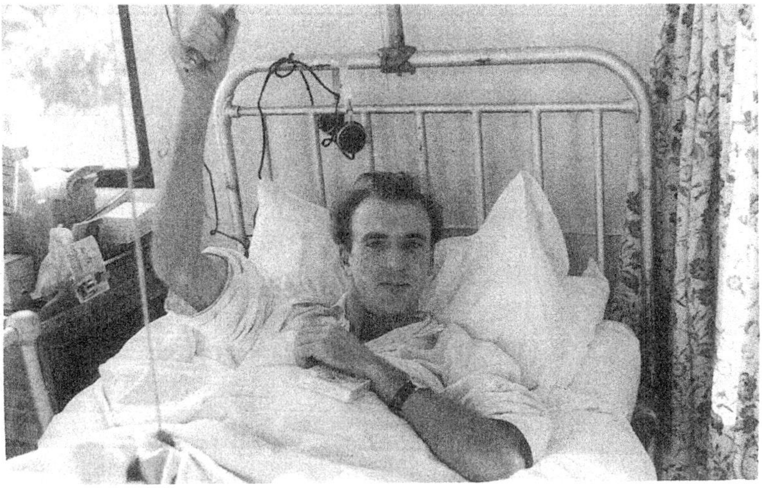

Recovering in hospital after the crash at Crystal Palace

A proud Bernard in later years with his trophy cabinet

GOLDIE

Gold Star Owners Club
UK Branch Newsletter

SEPTEMBER
1998

Bernard on cover of The Gold Star owners club newsletter

CHAPTER THIRTEEN

BERNARD'S ADVERSARIES

John Hartle

John Hartle was born in 1933 and lived in Chapel-en-le-Frith in the heart of the Peak District. After leaving school he worked at a local garage learning all aspects of the trade, but his main interest was always motorcycles. In his spare time, he would spectate at local trials and scrambles events but eventually he couldn't resist having a go himself. This was 1950 and he had also joined a local dealership that was sponsoring a couple of road racers, who he would help at meetings as their mechanic and generally assist in the pit.

In 1953 he made his racing debut at Brough Aerodrome riding a BSA, as well as meetings at Cadwell Park. Later in the year he rode an AJS 7R in the Junior Manx Grand Prix and a Manx Norton in the Senior. He crashed the 7R in the Junior event but restarted and finished 21st. He finished 15th in the Senior race and, as a result of these finishes, won the newcomers award that year. In 1954 he finished third in the Junior Manx Grand Prix on a new AJS 7R and he was leading the Senior race on a new Norton until he had to retire on the last lap. The same year he had some good results in the Hutchinson 100 which was held at Silverstone.

The Norton factory team could see the potential John had and invited him to join them and ride alongside John Surtees and Jack Brett. During the 1956 and 57 seasons he frequently raced against Bernard, with one notable meeting at Cadwell Park on August Bank Holiday 1957, where John broke four lap records (six- and eight-lap 350cc and 500cc records and equalled the 500cc single lap record). He also won both the 350cc final and the main event of the day, the "Coronation Trophy" final. Bernard, who was described that day as being in brilliant form, could not match the ex-works Norton. John rode for the MV Agusta factory team in 1958 and 1959 and in the 1960 TT where he won the Junior race and finished second in the Senior but was then - astonishingly - dismissed soon after.

He reverted to riding his own Norton as a privateer after that until he was recruited into the Scuderia Duke Gilera team on Gilera's return to racing in

1963. His last win was at the Dutch TT in the 500cc class in 1963. At the end of the season this team disbanded, and John went back to racing his own machines. By the mid-sixties he raced Aermacchi machines and in 1967 he started a business selling racing spares. He died on 31st August 1968 after a crash at Oliver's Mount Scarborough. He was 34 years old.

Bob McIntyre

Robert Macgregor McIntyre was born in Glasgow in 1928 and, after leaving school, worked at a local garage. His first motorcycle was a 1931 Norton. After he completed his national service, he bought an Ariel Red Hunter, which was his only form of transport, and soon started competing in off-road scramble events at local tracks. After spectating at a road race meeting at Kirkcaldy, Bob decided he wanted to try his hand on tarmac, so he entered a meeting at Balado Airfield near Kinross riding a borrowed BSA. The concrete track had patches of loose gravel, but with his experience of scrambles and off-road riding he excelled and won three of the four races he entered. In 1952 he was given the opportunity to race in the Clubman's TT on a BSA Gold Star, remarkably finishing second and also setting the fastest lap of the race, which was a new class record of 80.09mph. A few months later he entered the Junior Manx Grand Prix on a AJS 7R, won the race and also finished second in the Senior race on the same machine.

In 1953 he achieved his first international win at the North West 200 in the 350cc class on an AJS 7R. On the strength of this result, he was signed by the AJS team to compete in the 1953 World Championship. The only win he got was in France, but he did finish second in the Ulster Grand Prix and in the top six in Belgium, Switzerland, and the Netherlands. After this, AJS retired from racing, which left him riding 250cc, 350cc and 500cc Manx Nortons for Joe Potts, the Glasgow tuner.

This was the period in his career when he raced against Bernard at domestic meetings such as Thruxton and Cadwell Park. Bob was signed by the Gilera team in 1957 to race at the Jubilee TT on the factory-prepared four-cylinder machines, winning the double and achieving the first 100mph lap of the mountain course. Later in the year he broke the one-hour speed record at the banked Monza track riding a 350cc Gilera; he averaged 141mph, and this record stood until 1964 when Mike Hailwood achieved 144.8mph on an MV Agusta. Later in his career he rode for the Bianchi factory team and for Honda.

Bob still competed in non-Championship events, and at Oulton Park in August 1962 he won the 250cc race. After a bad start on his 499cc Norton in the 500cc event he had fought his way into the lead when he lost control of his machine on a wet patch of track and hit a post on an advertising board, sustaining a serious head injury. He was taken to hospital but died nine days later. He was 33 and had just become a father to Eleanor Campbell McIntyre on 18th July.

Alastair King

Alastair King was born in Killearn, Glasgow, in 1927 and was good friends with Bob McIntyre throughout their racing careers. His first race was at Errol Aerodrome in 1951 where he raced a Norton International to sixth place in the final. The following year he obtained a Velocette KTT Mark VIII. He found it difficult to compete against Manx Nortons and AJS 7Rs so for 1953 he bought a Norton International with a Featherbed frame and finished fifth in the Senior Clubman's TT with an average speed of 81.77mph and in 1954 he won the Senior Clubman's event on a BSA Gold Star.

The following year, 1955, was a disappointing year with injuries and mechanical problems and it was a blessing when the season was over. By contrast, 1956 was a completely different story: he raced against Bernard at Scarborough, Silverstone, Mallory Park, Oulton Park and, of course, Cadwell Park as well as the Manx Grand Prix, sharing the honours with Bernard on occasions. He achieved a new Junior lap record in the Manx Grand Prix on a Norton with a time of 24m 51.8sec, a speed of 91.07mph which stood for several years.

Alastair became teammates with Bob McIntyre for the 1957 season on Joe Potts's Nortons, winning his first TT Replica by finishing seventh in the Senior race. He raced the Nortons in 1958 as well, beating Geoff Duke at Oulton Park at the beginning of the year, but a crash at the TT in the Senior race resulted in three months away from racing to recuperate.

Easter Monday in 1958 at Oulton Park Alastair won the 250cc, 350cc and 500cc finals. It was only John Surtees on the MV Agusta that prevented him from winning more races in his career: for example, in the TT he finished third in the Junior race behind Surtees and Hartle on MV Agustas and second behind Surtees in the Senior.

There was not a great deal of success over the next few years, until 1961 when he finished third in the 500cc Ulster Grand Prix, second in the 350cc race, and fourth in the Senior TT. His best result in a World Championship round was a second place behind Mike Hailwood at Monza in the 500cc Italian Grand Prix in September.

After his good friend and countryman Bob McIntyre was tragically killed in August 1962 Alastair paraded Bob's Matchless G50 Special at a remembrance meeting at Oulton Park in October 1962 and then retired from motorcycle racing.

John Surtees

Probably the most talented and gifted rider Bernard raced against was John Surtees. Add to that the fact that Surtees often had superior machinery and it shows how good Bernard was to be able to compete regularly at that level. Born in 1934, John was the son of sidecar racer Jack Surtees. At the age of only fourteen John was passenger for his father in a sidecar event; they won but would later be disqualified because of John's age. His first official win came at the Aberdare Park Circuit in Wales when he was seventeen, riding a 499cc Vincent that he had built himself.

In 1955, John, John Hartle and Jack Brett were signed by Norton to ride works development Manx machines. John repaid Norton by winning the British Championship that year and to show how dominant he was in 1955 he won 68 of the 76 races he competed in. The following year he rode the four-cylinder MV Agusta in the World Championship events, but he also raced a pair of Nortons (348cc and 499cc) and MV Agusta or NSU machines in the 250cc class at domestic meetings where he competed against Bernard at Snetterton, Scarborough, the Isle of Man and Cadwell Park. They would not only race against each but often break each other's lap records, especially at Cadwell Park. He would sometimes compete on the MV Agusta at British meetings, the first time being at Crystal Palace in 1956.

His World Championship record is among the best with 500cc World titles in 1956, 1958, 1959 and 1960, finishing third in 1957, and 350cc World titles in 1958, 1959 and 1960.

In 1961 he decided to move into car racing. Initially he drove for Ken Tyrell and later for Colin Chapman's Lotus Team. He became a factory Ferrari driver for the 1963 and 1964 seasons winning the World drivers' Championship in 1964 and becoming the only man to be World Champion in Formula 1 and motorcycle racing's premier class, a feat that I doubt will ever be equalled. Once he had retired from racing, he developed his own Formula 1 team, giving Mike Hailwood the opportunity to drive one of his cars. The Formula 1 team was sold to Frank Williams in the late 70s. John died on 10th March 2017 at St. Georges Hospital, London aged 83.

George Catlin

I couldn't write a book about the racing career of Bernard Codd without mentioning George Catlin. They had some epic battles at tracks all over the country but especially at Cadwell Park, and while researching and writing this book I have been privileged to listen to some of the stories remembered by racing enthusiasts who were there on these exciting race days, and who witnessed first-hand the wheel-to-wheel dicing at speeds exceeding 100mph.

George, like Bernard, was the son of a Lincolnshire farmer. He was born in 1932 and started competitive motorcycle racing - as many riders did - with grass track and scrambling events in 1949. He soon had the urge to try his hand at road racing and Stan Hanson, a local businessman, could see his potential and decided to sponsor him and supplied two Manx Nortons, (348cc and a 499cc).

George lived in Minting, which is just up the road from Cadwell Park, so it was there that he would primarily learn his trade though he did race at Alton Towers and Osmaston Manor. In 1954 he entered the Manx Grand Prix riding his Nortons. He retired from the Junior race but finished a very creditable 25th out of 61 starters in the Senior. George raced against Bernard during the 1955, 1956 and 1957 seasons and as I have already mentioned they had some very close duels. They became and stayed good friends and they had a mutual respect, but they were both super competitive once the flag dropped and the racing started.

In 1958 George had a successful season with his best result at the TT with fifth place in the Junior and seventh in the Senior. He also won the Gold Cup at Oliver's Mount Scarborough. There was a change of sponsor in 1959 with Tom Arter providing him with a 349cc AJS 7R and a 498cc G50 Matchless. He would also race in the 250cc class on a 248cc NSU. George beat Bernard's long-standing six-lap 350cc record at Cadwell Park in May 1959 by 1.8 seconds. He also posted the fastest lap at 1m 10sec, which was 0.5sec faster than John Hartle's 1957 lap.

In 1961 at the Montlhery Circuit in France, George was part of a four-man team (Ellis Boyce, John Holder, Sid Mizen and George) that broke the 12- and 24-hour speed records. They posted an average speed of 109.39mph for the 12-hour record and 109.24mph for the 24-hour record, beating the existing record by almost 10mph and covering a total of 2,622 miles. Riding a 579cc BMW R69 S, the machine was prepared by the UK BMW dealer MLG and had a specially made dolphin fairing and modifications that included high compression pistons, long megaphones which incorporated silencers and a pad over the fuel tank to allow the rider to lay on the machine for long periods and still be comfortable. On April 28th, 2019, at the International Classic Motorcycle show held at Stafford Showground, a 1961 BMW 597cc R69 S reputedly to be the ex-MLG record breaking machine sold for £29,000.

Unlike Bernard, George was fortunate and had a reasonably long career in the sport without serious injury. After he retired from racing, he managed 'The Boston Motorcycling Centre' shop at 11 Red Lion Street, Boston before starting his own finance company, also in Boston. George died in 1992.

CHAPTER FOURTEEN

LIFE AFTER RACING

"He did not have much to show for his efforts"

Newspaper reports regarding Bernard are few and far between after he finished racing. There was one report that on Thursday 21st August 1958, Bernard and his brother Gerald were ushers at their sister's wedding. Miss Ena Margaret Codd was married at St. Mary & St. Nicholas Church, Wrangle.

Bernard was also present at the wedding of George Catlin to Sheila Maureen Walmsley on Monday 26th October 1959 at St. Nicholas Church Boston. Other motorcycling friends who attended included Jack Beeton (sidecar racer) from Louth, Jack Melhuish from Wragby and his passenger, Mr. T. Willerton.

The Louth Standard reported on January 1st, 1960, that Bernard had been to Brands Hatch with Jack Pitcher to compete in the Boxing Day car racing meeting. They travelled down on Christmas Day. It stated that Bernard was Jack's mechanic. Jack won the event in which he was entered.

On Friday 26th August 1960, The Louth Standard again reported on the fourth stockcar meeting that took place at Cadwell Park on Sunday 21st. The report said: *"Members of the Kart club competed in a number of events, Bernard Codd was driving a kart, but he did not have much to show for his efforts"*

Wednesday 4th January 1961 Bernard attended the funeral of Gordon Woodman who had been a big help and influence in the success of Bernard's racing career. Gordon was 53.

In 1962 Bernard attended the funeral of Peter Chatterton the racing motorcyclist who died in a tragic road accident near his home at the High Ferry Garage, Sibsey, near Boston. The funeral was at Sibsey Parish Church followed by cremation at Grimsby. Other motorcycling celebrities that attended the funeral included George Catlin, John Stancer, Derek Phillips, Ron Lilley, Austin Munks and Ted Wildman.

Bernard had returned to work on the family farm where he continued to live a more sedate lifestyle away from the noise and excitement of the racetrack and, on 28th September 1965, he married Miss Janet Owen at Holy Trinity Collegiate Church, Tattershall. As far as hobbies and pastimes were concerned, he turned his hand to golf and thoroughly enjoyed it until a neck problem put an end to that.

Sam Coupland, the man responsible for tuning Bernard's early racing machines, including the Clubman's TT winning BSA Gold Stars, passed away on 10th October 1977, aged 72.

Austin Munks, the person who first saw Bernard's potential and gave him the opportunity, first in Trials events and then in Road Racing, by providing the machinery for him to compete on, passed away on 29th January 1981, aged 73.

In 1988 Bernard was featured in 'Classic Motorcycling Legends' magazine alongside the great names in the sport from yesteryear and was portrayed on the front cover of 'Goldie', the Gold Star Owners Club UK newsletter in September 1998. He was also the subject of an article in 'Classic Bike' magazine in June 2005.

Mick Walker, the writer of numerous motorcycling books including, in 2004, 'The BSA Gold Star', featured Bernard in the book and mentioned him in the credits thanking him, amongst others, for their help.

In 2007 Bernard was asked to write the forward for the fascinating and very informative book 'The History of the Clubmans TT Races' by Fred Pidcock and Bill Snelling. A must-read for anyone at all interested in the story of the Clubmans event from day one until the final races in 1956.

June 30th, 2012 was the 75th anniversary of Walter Handley's 107mph lap of the Brooklands Circuit riding a modified BSA Empire Star. He was awarded a Brooklands Gold Star for his achievements. The BSA Company renamed the 'Empire Star' the 'Gold Star' in recognition of this event, which resulted in BSA starting production of the M24 Gold Star model the following year (1938) also in recognition of this event, thereby starting a legacy that dominated in its racing class for many years. There were 270 Gold Stars (including Rocket Gold Stars) attending the anniversary at the Brooklands Circuit and Bernard was invited as a guest of honour as he and his achievements were considered legendary by the Gold Star Owners Club.

Bernard finally settled on snooker and, with having the suitable out-buildings on the farm, had a full-sized snooker table installed where he could enjoy his new passion, achieving his highest break of forty-nine. He also kept a keen interest in modern-day motorcycle racing, especially the Moto GP races and Valentino Rossi in particular.

Even today as you look round the snooker room there are plenty of pictures and memories of those special times in Bernard's life that were so important to him and his family, and I hope after reading his racing story you will also appreciate what Bernard achieved, what a star he was, and what a superstar he so easily could have become.

Bernard passed away at home on Monday 29th July 2013, aged 79 years.

Mr Gerald White's bike that we believe to be the 350cc BSA Gold Star that Bernard won the Clubman's TT on, and which was bought by Gerald from Sam Coupland's motorcycle shop at Frithville in October 1956 (Still with Bernard's homemade knee and chin pads)

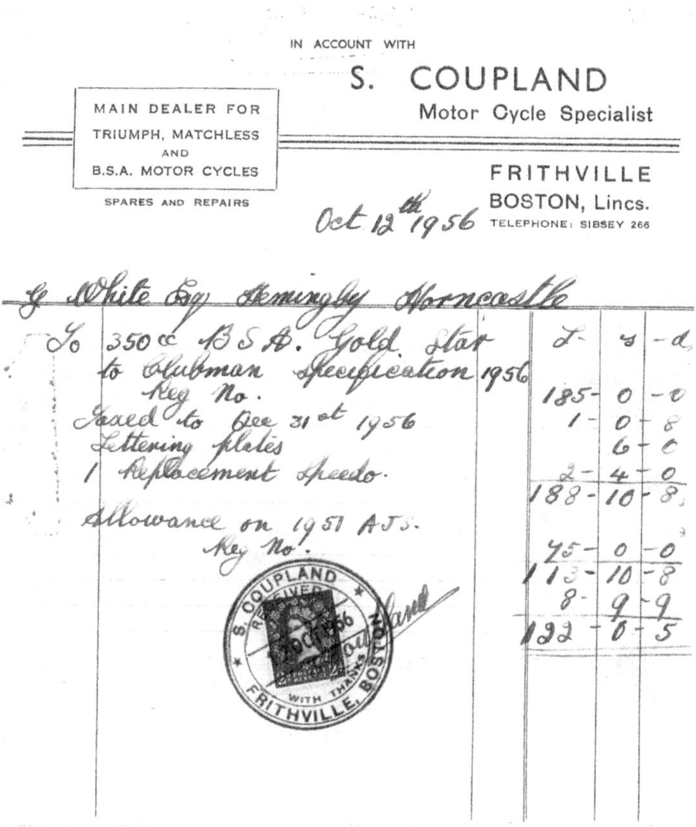

IN ACCOUNT WITH

S. COUPLAND
Motor Cycle Specialist

MAIN DEALER FOR
TRIUMPH, MATCHLESS
AND
B.S.A. MOTOR CYCLES

SPARES AND REPAIRS

FRITHVILLE
BOSTON, Lincs.
TELEPHONE: SIBSEY 266

Oct 12th 1956

G White Esq Hemingby Horncastle

	£	s	d
To 350cc B.S.A. Gold Star to Clubman Specification 1956 Reg No.	185	0	0
Taxed to Dec 31st 1956	1	0	8
Lettering plates		6	6
1 Replacement Speedo.	2	4	0
	188	10	8
Allowance on 1951 AJS. Reg No.	75	0	0
	113	10	8
	8	9	9
	122	0	5

S. COUPLAND RECEIVED 20 OCT 1956 WITH THANKS FRITHVILLE, BOSTON

S. Coupland

The bill of sale for the 350cc Gold Star (bike as yet unregistered)

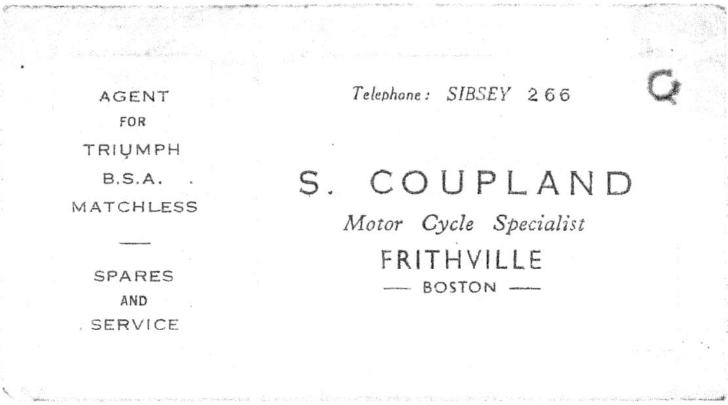

Sam Coupland's business card from the 1950s

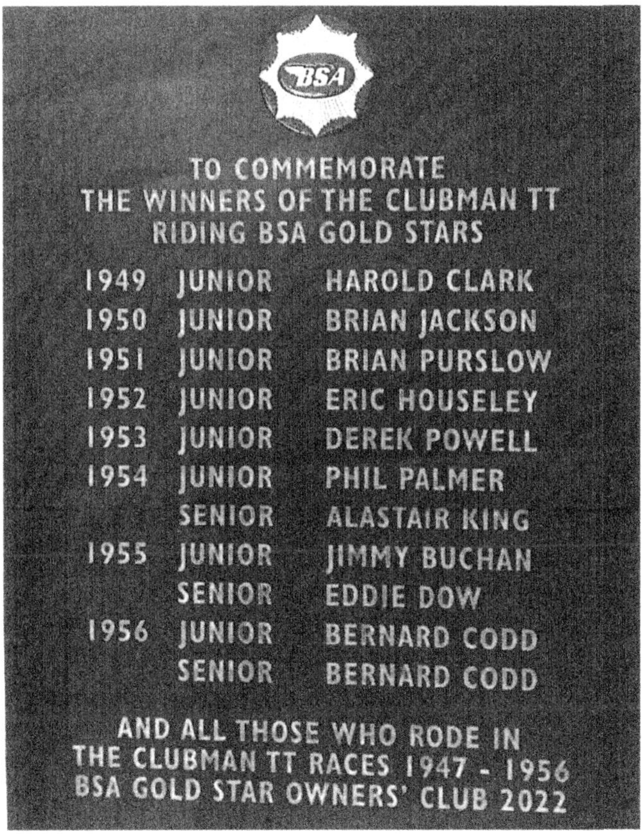

The plaque to commemorate the winners of the Clubmans TT events riding BSA Gold Stars

POSTSCRIPT

Just as I thought the book was complete and ready to go to print, I called to see Jane Codd to clarify one or two points. Whilst I was there, she informed me she had received a letter from Mr. Fred Pidcock of the BSA Gold Star Owners Club and co-author of 'The History of the Clubman's TT Races'. He explained that the memorial they had been erecting in Cumbria in memory of Walter Handley (the rider who achieved the gold star at Brooklands on 30th June 1937) was such a success and had generated such a lot of interest, that the BSA Owners club suggested putting a plaque in the Isle of Man to commemorate the BSA Gold Star riders who won the Clubman's TT Races between 1947 and 1956.

The plaque was to be positioned behind the main grandstand facing the scrutineering bay and it was planned to be unveiled on 24th August 2022 during the Manx GP race week. The plaque includes the names of Harold Clark, Brian Jackson, Brian Purslow, Eric Houseley, Derek Powell, Phil Palmer, Alastair King, Jimmy Buchan, Eddie Dow and - of course - Bernard Codd.

A fitting tribute to the domination of the BSA Gold Star and Bernard's personal achievements in this event. The BSA Gold Star was, after all, the machine that put Bernard's name in the motorcycling history books.

AFTERWORD

The TT winning BSA 350 Goldstar

Quite often, no one knows what happens to a race bike after the end of its racing career - especially one that raced almost 70 years ago; the bike is sold and disappears but, by an amazing coincidence, we do know what happened next to Bernard's Isle of Man winning 350 Goldstar that was tuned by Sam Coupland.

Jane Carrott, who jointly edited this book, was widowed soon after her first marriage but remained close to her in-laws, Ann and Gerald White, who lived all their lives in and around Horncastle. Jane later married Andy Carrott, who got to know Ann and Gerald very well. Andy had many chats with Gerald about the motorcycles that he rode when he was young. Gerald was a keen motorcyclist and had owned a variety of bikes including James and BSA, riding them for both work and pleasure. He would visit Cadwell Park, take part in local club events and even toured Scotland two-up on a 350 Matchless. He often spoke highly of his favourite bike, a 350 BSA Goldstar, purchased from Sam Coupland at Frithville near Boston and claimed to be a TT winner. Whilst editing this book Andy had a lightbulb moment: could this - just maybe - be Bernard's TT-winning bike?

Gerald, now 86 years old, suffers with dementia but, whilst he may be the first to admit he cannot remember what he had for lunch, he has vivid memories of his early life and confirmed that his bike was indeed the winning TT bike ridden by Bernard, stating only recently that *"it didn't half go!"*

If that evidence wasn't enough, we were able to compare a picture of the race bike with pictures in Gerald's collection. Although the bike was returned to road trim it was still sporting what appear to be home-made knee pads fitted for racing. Gerald also has a letter from Sam Coupland with details of the deal that included fitting a speedometer (which would have been removed for racing).

The bike's winning streak did not end at the TT: as a keen rider, Gerald entered and won a Banovallum Club Road trial on the Goldstar and still has the trophy, along with the details of the route.

Gerald was, like Bernard, a member of the Banovallum Motorcycle Club in Horncastle, as were both of Gerald's brothers-in-law, Mike Baldwin and Mo Ruhier. Mike and Mo were both fans of Bernard and were able to corroborate Gerald's story about the 350. All three would regularly watch Bernard and his contemporaries at Cadwell Park. Quite some years later Mike and Mo visited an exhibition at the Museum of Lincolnshire Life. As they poured over many black-and-white photographs of Cadwell Park, they remarked on a particular picture of Bernard Codd. As they were reminiscing, a voice behind them interrupted their discussion. It was none other than Bernard himself! They were honoured to meet one of their racing heroes and had a lengthy chat, during which Bernard confirmed that he had, indeed, been offered the chance to ride for Gilera. In researching this book, it had not been possible to prove a connection between Bernard and Gilera but now, not only had we found one of Bernard's bikes, but we also found two people who were told by the man himself that Gilera had offered him a chance to ride their bikes.

Unfortunately, we have no record of who purchased the BSA from Gerald, but he said that he had sold it to someone at Syston, near Grantham. There is no record of the bike on the DVLA database.

Printed in Great Britain
by Amazon

34135724R00116